Take Control with Your

401(k)

An Employee's Guide to Maximizing Your Investments

D A V I D   L .   W R A Y

President, Profit Sharing/401(k) Council of America

Dearborn™
Trade Publishing
A **Kaplan Professional** Company

JUN 2002

This publication is designed to provide accurate and authoritative information in regard to the subject matter covered. It is sold with the understanding that the publisher is not engaged in rendering legal, accounting, or other professional service. If legal advice or other expert assistance is required, the services of a competent professional should be sought.

Editorial Director: Donald J. Hull
Senior Project Editor: Trey Thoelcke
Interior Design: Lucy Jenkins
Cover Design: Scott Rattray, Rattray Designs
Typesetting: the dotted i

Library of Congress Cataloging-in-Publication Data

Wray, David L.
　　Take control with your 401(k) : an employee's guide to maximizing your investments / David L. Wray.
　　　　p.　　cm.
　　Includes index.
　　ISBN 0-7931-5411-1
　　1. 401(k) plans. 2. Individual retirement accounts—United States. 3. Pension trusts—United States. 4. 401(k) plans—Taxation—Law and legislation.
5. Individual retirement accounts—Taxation—Law and legislation—United States. 6. Pension trusts—Taxation—Law and legislation—United States.
7. Old age pensions—Taxation—Law and legislation—United States.
8. Retirement income—United States. 9. Retirement income—Taxation—United States. 10. United States. Economic Growth and Tax Relief Reconciliation Act of 2001. I. Title.
HD7105.45.U6 W73 2002

　　　　　　　　　　　　　　　　　　　　　　　　　　　2002002081

Contents

Preface

How do you imagine your dream retirement? Are you relaxing in the sunshine on a sandy beach? Do you see yourself traveling from resort to resort or playing in a seniors' tennis tournament? Are you volunteering for the Peace Corps? Or are your grandchildren eagerly visiting you at your beautiful retirement home? Stop dreaming! This is not just a fantasy. Your dreams and those of every American can become real with 401(k).

This book is the practical tool and information guide that will make your retirement dreams come true. But before we begin building your retirement success, there's something you need to know: This golden time of retirement has not always existed. Whether sitting behind a desk or hunting and gathering, human beings have historically worked until they died. When the Social Security retirement age was set at 65 years old, few were expected to live long enough to collect—and as recently as the 1930s, nearly all Americans did pass away before they could retire. But the constant life-changing improvements begun in the 20th century are affecting more than just science and industry. These dynamic changes are allowing new freedoms and possibilities. In addition to a longer life span and a better quality of living, you are also enjoying an entirely new philosophy of employment—working to live, not living to work.

We have been given the opportunity to throw off the limited thinking of the past and go where people have not gone before, especially in our golden years. However, each of us is responsible for making these new possibilities a reality. With life spans now pushing 100 years or more, future retirees may spend several decades in retirement, and many whose retirement is based on early models will be caught unprepared. New retirement realities call for new approaches. Fortunately, a wonderful tool has been developed to help you accomplish your dreams—your 401(k) plan.

The 401(k) Way

Traditional retirement approaches assumed two things: (1) Retirees would not live long; and (2) Retirees would need much less money in retirement. Under these assumptions, low monthly pension payments and Social Security would be enough to keep retirees going. Because the time frame for these payments was expected to be just a few years, the expense to the system would be minimal. But all this has changed. In the twenty-first century, retirees can expect to be healthy and live for 20 years or more after retirement. Retirement is now about enjoying your final years, not just watching television in a retirement home. Because we will continue to lead active lives, we will all need at least 70 percent of our preretirement income.

While the government still provides a foundation of retirement income, growing numbers of Americans are turning to 401(k) plans to ensure their financial success. By the end of 2000, there were nearly 35 million Americans participating in more than 350,000 401(k) plans—a huge increase from 1984 when there were only 17,000 plans with 7.5 million participants. These numbers continue to rise as more and more people request that their companies offer 401(k) plans.

Don't worry. This is not a trend or a fashionable fad. The government will not suddenly take 401(k) plans away or decrease their benefits. In fact, both the government and your employer want 401(k) to stick around. Employers use 401(k) to add satisfaction to your employment relationship and reward you for staying longer at the company, while the government (which wants you to have enough in retirement) has been increasing 401(k) limits. Basically, all aspects of the system—employers, employees, and the government—have recognized the power of 401(k).

So why are 401(k) plans so popular and financially successful? The 401(k) way is based on two simple principles: taking control of your retirement and becoming a lifetime investor.

Taking Control = Having It Your Way

We're all familiar with the advertising slogan "have it your way." The expectation of getting a specialized item tailor-made to fit the individual, rather than a generic product made for the masses, typifies the way Americans think. We like freedom and choices. Unfortunately, for a long time we were receiving the equivalent of mass-produced food when it came to paying for retirement.

Then 401(k) came onto the scene. 401(k) perfectly fills this need because it is not designed for one specific type of investor. It can be simple or sophisticated; hands-on or hands-off. If you have a lot of time to customize and care for your retirement plan, 401(k) will let you. If you want to spend as little time as possible on your 401(k) approach, you can do that too. Think of 401(k) as a tool that can be personalized to fit everyone's different needs. Regardless of what your goal is and how you want to attain it, 401(k) will work for you.

Why settle for a one-size-fits-all retirement plan that may provide you with far less than you need? Once you take control, you can relax knowing you have a very comfortable future ahead—one that is right just for you.

Lifetime Investors Beat Inflation

Here's the bad news: Because retirees will be living so much longer, your biggest financial risk is inflation. You may save a considerable amount of money when you are younger, but your purchasing power will decrease every year due to inflation. For example, 3 percent inflation (the typical rate) halves the value of your money in 24 years. In the 1960s, a fast food hamburger cost just 15 cents. Today it will cost you $1. While 85 cents is not a huge increase, the *percentage* of the increase is an indication of how much items will cost in 40 years—6.6 times more! Consider how much big-ticket items such as appliances, cars, clothes, and trips will cost 40 years down the line. In order to keep up with this rise in costs, your money has to grow as well.

But here's the good news: 401(k) plans do not simply keep up with inflation, they beat it. Because 401(k) assets are invested for the long term they ride out the general ups and downs of the market, earning a steady average return over the years. Thanks to this long-term increase in your assets (along with pretax contributions and an employer match) you will definitely come out ahead when you retire. Ever heard of a 401(k) millionaire? Ever thought of becoming one yourself?

What This Book Will Do for You

Are you ready to take control of your financial future and become a lifetime investor? If you're like me, now that you have a glimpse of the success that is in your reach, you are ready to grab it.

Think of a 401(k) plan as a retirement vehicle; in other words, it is a car you can drive to your retirement goal. If you have not already joined your company's plan, the time to get behind the wheel of your 401(k) is now. This book will provide you with all the mechanics of your car, a traveler's guide to help you pick the best retirement destination, and a road map that shows how to get where you're going. All you have to do is get the motor humming by signing up and starting to save.

Some of the questions this book will answer are:

- How do 401(k) plans save me money on taxes?
- How can I make my money grow?
- How much money will I need in retirement?
- Why is a company match so great?
- How do I get my money out in an emergency?
- How can I avoid big fees and paperwork?
- How do I choose the right investments?
- How does long-term investing work?
- What happens when I retire?

Remember: You're in the driver's seat. You're in control. Ready? Set. Go!

Acknowledgments

I could not have written *Take Control with Your 401(k)* without much support, past and present.

I especially want to thank my daughter, Amy Wray, who partnered with me every step of the way. Her contributions as writer, editor, and cheerleader were the mortar that held this project together.

I extend my deepest thanks to the following people whose input took the book to another level:

- G. Dawn Anderson
- Karen Kay Barnes
- Michael Falk
- Kevin Feeney
- David A. Hildebrandt
- Linda P. Holleman
- Michael P. Kelso
- Judy Knoll
- Ian S. Kopelman
- Thomas J. Mess
- Bruce Musselman
- Douglas G. Prince
- Kenneth A. Raskin
- Timothy J. Regnitz
- Allan W. TeRonde
- Sheryl L. Wright

I also extend my profound gratitude to the members of PSCA's staff:

- Patricia A. Alman
- Matthew Collings
- Edward Ferrigno
- Georgianne S. Mudie
- Connie M. Mullis
- Debra R. Schloesslin
- Elizabeth L. Nevins

I want to thank C. Clarke Imbler who introduced me to 401(k) in 1982 and Theodore D. Bower who spent 1987 teaching me all about ERISA.

Finally, I want to thank my wife, Judy, for her encouragement and her tolerance of my absence on so many weekends.

401(k)
What's It All About?

According to the legal definition, a *401(k)* is a retirement savings program provided by your employer in which your savings are not immediately subject to federal income taxes and in many cases state income taxes. But it is also much more. Your 401(k) plan is a great retirement savings choice that provides benefits no other plan offers, making it the most successful retirement plan available today.

Throughout this book you will learn in detail why 401(k) is such a beneficial option and you will find out exactly what you need to make your 401(k) plan work for you. But to get you started and whet your appetite for more, here's the essence of 401(k) plans—a "best of" list that highlights the top eight reasons why you should participate in your 401(k).

Eight Reasons Why 401(k) Is Right for You

1. *In a 401(k) plan, you decide how much of your paycheck to save.* You chose the contribution amount, up to the government's generous maximum ($11,000 in 2002). And this maximum increases annually: In 2006, the maximum will be $15,000 for regular savers or a $20,000 maximum contribution if you are over 50 years old.
2. *401(k) saving is effortless.* Your employer will automatically deduct from your paycheck the amount you choose to put away, saving you the time and effort necessary to open an individual savings account.
3. *401(k) makes investing easy.* You invest your money in funds you choose from investment options prescreened by your

employer, saving you time and expense, while reducing risk. Or your employer may invest your money for you, making it even easier.

4. *Your savings are increased by your employer's matching contribution.* The average employer matches 50 percent of your contribution, or 50 cents for every $1 you save.

5. *Contributions to 401(k) accounts take place pretax.* This means you can invest much more because the government doesn't impose income taxes until the money is withdrawn. This also means the growth of your investments will be on a larger pool of money than in an after-tax plan, and you might reduce your income tax bracket as well.

6. *Earnings are also tax-sheltered.* Because 401(k) plan investment earnings are reinvested without immediate taxation, the account can grow at a considerably accelerated rate.

7. *Investments are long term.* By investing your money over many years, as you do in a 401(k) plan, you can receive a far greater rate of return than you could in any passbook savings account.

8. *Your 401(k) account belongs to you.* When you change jobs you take the money with you in the form of a rollover to your new employer's 401(k) plan or a rollover to another tax shelter, such as an IRA.

I can boil it down even further, to just one word: growth. 401(k) plans are the right choice for anyone who wishes to have a successful retirement because these plans allow for incredible growth. In fact, the growth opportunities of the 401(k) plan are so impressive that both the federal government and your employer support them.

It's a Win-Win World

You'd heard that 401(k) plans are a fast, efficient way to save for retirement, offering the most control and the best investment options. Now you know that it's true. 401(k) plans allow you to save money on a pretax basis at the highest limit available, your contributions will often be matched by employer funds, and your long-term investment horizon will really pay off. But you still wonder: What's the catch?

Before you start combing the fine print looking for strings, special clauses, and pitfalls, let me save you some trouble. The 401(k) plan is the genuine article, a saving and investing vehicle that your employer wholeheartedly supports. No matter when you start participating, how much you put aside, or how you decide to invest, the 401(k) plan can only help you with your retirement goals. And your company is doing its best to help as well. In fact, if your company offers a match, it is actually rewarding you every time you save.

Are you *still* suspicious? Perhaps you're wondering exactly why your company is so supportive and what they are getting from this deal. Well, you're right to think that there are employer advantages to the 401(k) plan. By offering a 401(k) plan, your company gets a huge benefit—satisfied, high-quality workers like you.

On one hand, your employer wants high-quality, dedicated workers like yourself because you ensure company success. On the other hand, high turnover leads to high costs in finding and training new employees. So your company is both saving money and improving company success when it keeps you happy. How can it do that? It does so by giving you what you want—a savings plan that provides more growth of your money, more control, and lowers taxes. 401(k) plans are a win-win solution.

It's a whole new world of employer-employee relations, with 401(k) plans as just one of the goodwill ambassadors now being offered by companies. These plans are part of an employer-employee partnership helping American workers build personal wealth and create a financially secure retirement.

The Employer-Employee Partnership

Since the industrial revolution, when work began moving from the farm to offices and factories, there have been two main theories of employee management. If you haven't experienced these directly, I am sure you can imagine how it felt to be working under each mind-set:

- Workers are components to be trained to perform in a standardized way, under strict supervision. This is the philosophy of hierarchy from the top down, where owners/managers expect workers to do what they're told.
- Workers and owners/managers are adversaries in a constant struggle for advantage, with strikes and power plays on both sides.

Today there's a better way—the employer-employee partnership.

Many companies have a history of partnership with their employees. Since 1904, the Procter & Gamble Company has offered some kind of employer-sponsored savings plan to empower workers. The result of such plans is a happier work force, a stronger connection of workers to company goals, a more efficient work ethic, and a competitive edge for the company in the marketplace. The value of cooperation between employers and employees has been its own advertisement, and such plans are now widely used by employers to attract high-quality workers, motivate their already existing workers, and keep them on staff. In essence, 401(k) plans promote a win-win atmosphere for success.

In addition, the practice of offering 401(k) or other employer-based savings plans is about to explode onto the world economy. International competition has focused attention on quality, as well as price and quantity. Technology is increasing productivity, making each worker a bigger part of company success. The inefficient practice of limiting job responsibility and surrounding workers with expensive supervisors can't ensure success in today's rapidly changing marketplace.

The future is participation, cooperation, inclusion, partnership, self-management, individual responsibility, and shared decision making. Thanks to your employer, you now have the freedom, opportunity, and information you need to achieve your retirement goals.

Your 401(k) Checklist

So how do you use 401(k) to make your retirement dreams come true? These ten simple steps will take you where you want to be.

Copy this list and post it on the fridge, near your desk, or anywhere it will remind you that you are in charge of your retirement future.

1. *Take control.* Only you can ensure that you'll have enough money saved for your retirement.
2. *Know what you'll need.* Experts estimate that you'll need at least 70 percent of your preretirement income to maintain the same standard of living once you stop working. Your retirement income will need to last many years. If you retire at age 55, you can expect to live at least another 25 years.
3. *Start now.* Time is on your side. The sooner you start, the longer your money has to grow. It's never too early to start saving for a secure retirement.
4. *Participate.* The employer-sponsored 401(k) plan is convenient, easy to use, and one of the best retirement savings deals out there. Join today!
5. *Contribute to the max.* The more money you put in a 401(k) plan, the more you'll get out—especially because many companies match part or all of their employees' retirement contributions.
6. *Invest pretax.* Saving pretax gives you more money to invest. Because taxes take a large bite out of each dollar you earn, you have to save more after-tax dollars to get the same impact as pretax saving. Plus, saving pretax lowers your taxable income, which means that you'll pay less to the IRS on April 15th. The government also offers an extra tax incentive for lower income workers: Until the end of year 2005, you may be eligible to receive a tax credit of up to $1,000 when you save in a 401(k).
7. *Pay yourself first.* Out of sight, out of mind. You won't miss the money you're saving if it's deposited straight into your 401(k) plan, and the government, your employers, and your creditors won't be able to touch it.
8. *Keep your hands off.* Don't touch your retirement savings. You'll not only avoid tax penalties for using the money early, you'll also give your investments more time to grow. Don't take a loan or withdrawal from your 401(k) plan unless it's

a real emergency. And if you change jobs, rollover any amount you receive.

9. *Look long term.* Low-risk investments usually mean low returns and may put your retirement finances in danger down the line. For successful saving, choose investments that will beat inflation over the long haul.

10. *Be flexible.* As the years go by, life changes. So should your retirement savings strategy. Review it annually to ensure it still meets your needs as retirement approaches.

Continue reading to find out more about each of these ten steps and how they work!

2

The 401(k) Advantage

401(k) plans are one of the most popular and successful methods of saving for retirement, full of advantages that your employer and the government work together to provide. But for you to get the full benefit from your 401(k), you need to be aware of all the advantages and know exactly how to use them.

The 401(k) advantages break down into four basic components:

1. *Less tax pain, more gain.* The more you save and invest in your 401(k) plan, the greater your reward.
2. *Saving is easy.* 401(k) plans make saving for retirement simple and automatic.
3. *You're in control.* 401(k) plans give you control of the when, where, and how of your money.
4. *It's protected.* Both your employer and the government are responsible for making sure that your 401(k) savings are secure.

If this seems like a conspiracy to help you build a successful retirement, it is! The 401(k) plan is designed by employers and the government to help everyone get the best return on his or her investment dollar, and as a result be financially secure in retirement.

Less Tax Pain, More Gain

Pretax Contributions and Tax-Deferred Earnings

401(k) contributions are made pretax, which means that when your money goes into the plan it is not subject to federal income tax or most state and local income taxes. Likewise, investment earnings on your savings are not taxed until they are withdrawn from the plan. Because taxes take a large bite out of each dollar you earn, you have to save more after-tax dollars to get the same result as pretax saving. Thanks to pretax contributions, you are paying yourself rather than the government, and your assets multiply dramatically over time as investment returns compound on a larger pool of assets.

Let's assume that Pat and Gerry each start out earning $25,000 per year. Both would like to save 6 percent of their salary, or $1,500. Gerry is saving her contributions pretax in a 401(k), while Pat is saving in an after-tax vehicle, which means his $1,500 is hit by a 20 percent federal tax before it goes into his account. Both Gerry and Pat receive an 8 percent rate of return and can expect a 2.5 percent pay increase every year. At the end of 30 years, Pat would have $136,319, while Gerry would have saved $224,014—almost twice as much—as illustrated in Figure 2.1.

FIGURE 2.1   Difference in Pretax and After-Tax Investments

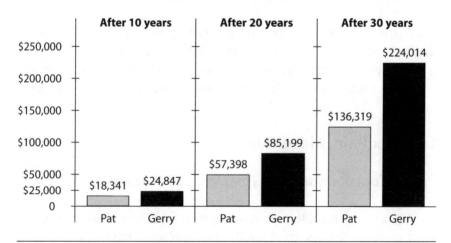

Assumptions: Gerry—Pre-Tax Investment   Pat—After-Tax Investment
              Starting salary—$25,000   Contribution—6 percent of pay
              Time span—30 years   Rate of return—8 percent
              Salary increase—2.5 percent per year
              Tax rate on after-tax contributions—20 percent

401(k) contributions lower your adjusted gross income for federal income tax purposes. Any contributions you make to your 401(k) reduce your taxable income. If you pay 20 percent of your salary in federal income taxes and you contribute $1,500 in pretax money, you save $300 on federal income taxes alone. In most cases, your 401(k) contributions also reduce the amount you have to pay in state income taxes. In addition, your contributions may drop you down into a lower tax bracket, reducing your overall tax rate as well. So be sure to use your reduced W-2 income as your taxable wages and earnings on your income tax form when tax time rolls around.

Supersized Savings

You can save a lot in your 401(k), and the level of maximum contribution is set to increase considerably over the next few years. In addition, the maximum contribution that you can make to your 401(k) is much greater than the maximum contribution to an IRA. In 2002, you can contribute at most $2,500 in an IRA, but the federal maximum contribution for 401(k) plans will be $11,000. Figure 2.2 details the 401(k) contribution limits for the next few years.

Not only are contribution limits getting higher all the time, plan-imposed restrictions required by government regulations limiting the percentage of pay you can allocate to retirement savings have been eased. Under the old rules, most employees were limited to contributing no more than 15 percent of pay to their 401(k) plan. So if you earned $50,000 in 2001, you could only stash $7,500 in

---

FIGURE 2.2   401(k) Contribution Limits

Year	Total Allowable Contributions
2002	$11,000
2003	$12,000
2004	$13,000
2005	$14,000
2006	$15,000

After 2006, contributions will be indexed to inflation by $500 increments every year following.

---

your company retirement plan even though the federal dollar limit was $10,500. Only 11 percent of plan participants maxed out their 401(k) contributions in 1999, according to a study by the Employee Benefits Research Institute. More than half of those who didn't were prohibited from doing so by their plan-imposed limits.

In 2002, it became a whole new story. Changes to federal law now permit employers to allow employees to contribute a higher percentage of their salary. Except for highly paid workers who face other restrictions, most employees can contribute the full dollar maximum ($11,000 in 2002) to their 401(k) plans. If you are 50 or older, you may be able to kick in an extra $1,000 per year—a welcome incentive as you approach retirement.

Tax Credit for Low-Income and Moderate-Income Savers

You may be eligible to claim a tax credit of up to $1,000 when you make contributions to your 401(k) plan, 403(b) plan, government 457 plan, SIMPLE, SEP, traditional IRA, or Roth IRA. After-tax contributions to qualified employer plans are also eligible. The tax credit for low-income and moderate-income savers (or "saver's credit") goes into effect at the beginning of 2002 and is scheduled to end after the 2005 taxable year. This credit applies only as a reduction to your income tax liability, not as cash in hand via a refund. If you owe no federal income tax, you are not eligible for a tax credit.

In order to qualify for the saver's credit you must be:

- 18 years of age or older
- Not a full-time student
- Not claimed as a dependent on someone else's return

In addition, you must meet one of the following financial criteria:

- File your taxes singly with an income of $25,000 or less
- File your taxes as head of household and have an income of $37,500 or less
- File your taxes jointly with an income of $50,000 or less

The tax credit ranges from 10 to 50 percent of each $1 you contribute, up to the first $2,000 you put in your 401(k). If you and your spouse both contribute to a 401(k) plan, you may both be eligible to receive a credit. The amount of your tax credit depends on the amount of your adjusted gross income. The income limits and applicable credit rate allowance are as shown in Figure 2.3.

The tax credit is in addition to other favorable tax treatment of the contribution, such as the deferral of income tax on pretax contributions. The credit is reduced by the taxable distributions you or your spouse receives from any plans eligible for the credit during the year the credit is claimed.

The credit is incredibly valuable for lower-income individuals, particularly if their employer matches their 401(k) contribution. Let's compare Pat and Gerry. They are both single tax filers and earn identical salaries of $15,000. Pat declines to take advantage of his employer's 401(k) plan while Gerry elects to contribute 3 percent of her earnings. Their employer offers a 50 percent match on the first 6 percent of compensation contributed by employees. Figure 2.4 details the effects of the tax credit and matching contribution on each person's net income.

While Pat's net income exceeded Gerry's by $158, she has $675 in her 401(k) plan compared to Pat's zero. How is this possible? Gerry's $450 401(k) contribution was replaced by her tax credit and her employer's match. She also lowered her adjusted gross income by $450, and as a result paid $67 less in tax at the 15 percent rate.

FIGURE 2.3 Tax Credit for Different Income Levels

Credit	Single Filers	Adjusted Gross Income Head of Household	Joint Filers
50% of contribution	0–$15,000	0–$22,500	0–$30,000
20% of contributions	$15,000–$16,250	$22,501–$24,375	$30,001–$32,500
10% of contributions	$16,251–$25,000	$24,376–$37,500	$32,501–$50,000
Credit not available	more than $25,000	more than $37,500	more than $50,000

FIGURE 2.4   Effect of Tax Credit and Matching Contribution on Net Income

	Pat	Gerry	Gerry's 401(k)
Annual Income	$15,000	$15,000	
401(k) Contribution Percent	0%	3%	
401(k) Contribution	$0	($450)	$450
Adjusted Gross Income	$15,000	$14,550	
2002 Tax Liability	($836)	($769)	
Add in the 50% tax credit	$0	$225	
Disposable Income*	$14,164	$14,006	
Employer match (50%)			$225
Net Total	$14,164	$14,006	$675

*Disregards FICA, FUTA, and state income tax

Gerry was required to reduce her daily spending by 43.3 cents to build a real retirement nest egg.

The government established this program because it wants to reward low-income and moderate-income workers who save for retirement. Not only do you receive up to a $1,000 deduction from the federal income taxes you owe, in many cases you will also get an employer matching contribution of 50 percent of the money you put into your plan. In other words, if you save $1, the government gives you 50 cents back and your employer puts 50 cents into your account. That's free money.

Matching Contributions

401(k) plans may offer a *company match*, which means your company makes a contribution to your plan whenever you do, usually about 50 cents on the dollar (depending on your plan). This is like a huge year-end bonus, and it is doubly valuable because matching contributions (and your investment earnings on them) are tax-sheltered within your 401(k) plan.

How much of a benefit is a 401(k) match? It's bigger and better than you think. Fifty cents for every dollar you contribute may sound like spare change, but over the years it really adds up. Then factor in that you will receive investment returns on the money you've invested *and* the money your company has added. These two benefits together help your 401(k) account grow by leaps and bounds.

Remember Pat and Gerry? Let's say they are still earning a starting salary of $25,000 and contributing 6 percent of pay, or $1,500. They are still earning an 8 percent rate of return, they can expect a 2.5 percent salary increase every year, and their time horizon is still 30 years. In this example, however, they are both putting their money away pretax in a 401(k). The big difference in their plans is that Pat receives a company match of 50 cents for every dollar up to 6 percent of pay, while Gerry's plan has no match. Gerry will have as much as she did in our previous example ($224,014 after 30 years), but Pat's company match has catapulted him past Gerry to a retirement account of $336,021. That's a $112,00 difference for merely being a participant in the plan. Figure 2.5 shows the results of both plans.

Lower Investment Management Fees

One of the advantages of a 401(k) plan is that you will pay lower fees than you would investing on your own. This is called an

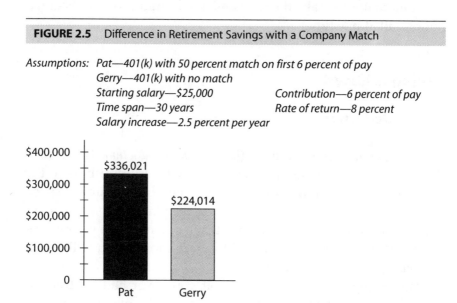

FIGURE 2.5   Difference in Retirement Savings with a Company Match

Assumptions: Pat—401(k) with 50 percent match on first 6 percent of pay
Gerry—401(k) with no match
Starting salary—$25,000   Contribution—6 percent of pay
Time span—30 years   Rate of return—8 percent
Salary increase—2.5 percent per year

economy of scale. Within your 401(k), your money is part of a pool made up of all the assets from the participants from your company. In contrast to the typical investment in an IRA, you typically pay lower investment management fees and you usually will not pay front-end or back-end sales commissions on investment purchases and sales through your 401(k) plan. In addition, employers may pay some or all of these costs, increasing your return. Your plan may also have a package arrangement with your service provider for specific services, such as balance transfers via an 800 number or over the Internet, and investment newsletters. Because you are one of many, your personal account receives individual management and administration at a lower overall cost.

Another advantage of the economy of scale is the stable flow of contributions. The large number of employees from your plan all make individual contributions, but when they are sent to your service provider they arrive via a single source—your employer. Your service provider can then efficiently combine and allocate the money once rather than numerous times. For example, for a 401(k) plan with 500 employees the provider will predictably receive a check every payroll period for the contributions of all the participants in that company's 401(k) plan. The provider can then use a computer program that will make the investment allocations of those contributions all at one time.

Saving Is Easy

Payroll Deduction

You save money in your 401(k) by *payroll deduction.* This means that once you designate the amount you wish to contribute to the plan, your employer will deduct the money from your paycheck every paycheck period and deposit it in the plan for you. Consider your 401(k) contributions to be mortgage payments on your retirement. After 30 years of paying a little each month, you will own a financially secure retirement.

The saying "you never miss what you never had" is true for 401(k) saving. Why? You are less likely to spend, plan to spend, or wish you could spend those funds on anything other than your 401(k). Payroll deduction makes everything automatic, reducing paperwork and eliminating your chances of forgetting to contribute. Using payroll deduction means one less financial worry.

No Minimum Contribution Requirements

Because there is no federally required minimum contribution to a 401(k) plan, you can save as little or as much as you want. For example, it is perfectly ok if you can only save 1 percent of your income, which could be $20 a month from a salary of $24,000 a year. Also, there is no minimum on the amount you can invest on each of the funds in your plan. For example, it is permissible for you to divide your $20 a month evenly among four different funds, resulting in a monthly investment of $5 in each fund. No other investment program works this easily.

Automatic Investment

Once you have determined how your 401(k) account will be invested, your savings will be automatically invested as you have directed every time your contributions are deposited into the plan. After your very first contribution you will begin to earn returns on your investments. Because you don't have to call a broker, initiate a financial transfer, or continually make decisions, your 401(k) makes investing easy.

Dollar Cost Averaging

Using your 401(k) payroll deduction to save, you are investing a fixed amount in your portfolio at regular intervals throughout the year. This results in an investment practice called *dollar cost averaging.* Dollar cost averaging means you are investing the same amount of money on a regular schedule rather than making one big investment. If the price of your chosen investment changes—which is always happening with the share price of stocks or stock mutual funds—you automatically buy more shares when the price is lower and fewer shares when it increases. By investing via dollar cost averaging you ensure that the cost of your shares is at the long-term average price, which reduces the uncertainty of short-term market volatility.

While the stock market ebbs and flows, you remain constant and steady. This means you never have to worry about incorrectly timing the market by purchasing all your stock at too high a price. For example, suppose you would like to buy shares of a stock that is particularly hot at the moment. Because everyone would like to own some of this stock, the cost per share rises to $10, costing you $6,000 for 600 shares. If you would have used dollar cost averaging and invested in the same stock every month with an amount of money that remained constant over the entire year, you could have purchased 895 shares for an average of $6.70 per share rather than 600 shares at $10 each. This dollar cost averaging approach is detailed in Figure 2.6.

FIGURE 2.6   Dollar Cost Averaging

Money to spend: $6,000, or $500 per month

Month	Price Per Share		Shares Purchased
January	$10		50.0
February	$12.50		40.0
March	$10		50.0
April	$ 8		62.5
May	$ 8		62.5
June	$ 8		62.5
July	$ 5		100.0
August	$ 4		125.0
September	$ 6.25		80.0
October	$ 5		100.0
November	$ 5		100.0
December	$ 8		62.5
Average Cost	$ 6.70	Total Shares	895

Screened Investment Choices

When you invest in your 401(k), you are not forced to choose your investments from the thousands of choices listed in the *Wall Street Journal*. The advantage of 401(k) is that your employer has researched and carefully considered all the options in order to provide you with a limited number of high-quality investment choices. Investing comes complete with its own language, rules, and thousands of alternatives. This is intimidating and may lead to poor choices. Having only a few employer-screened investments from which to choose simplifies your investment decision and greatly improves the likelihood of your financial success. Your employer may invest your money for you, which makes 401(k) investing even easier.

You Know What You Have

401(k) makes it easy to know what you have. Because 401(k) savings are in your own account, you can track your contributions, your employer's matching contributions, and the effects of your investment's return on your 401(k) assets. Typically, your employer will provide you with quarterly statements reporting activity in your 401(k) account. Increasingly, such information is also available via your company's telephone response system, intranet system or on the Internet, from which you can access your account via a PIN number of your choosing.

You're in Control

Contribution Flexibility

Your 401(k) plan allows you to save the amount that is right for you. Your contribution can be just 1 percent of pay. For example, if you are making $36,000 a year, you can contribute as little as $30 each month. On the other hand, you could save as much as the full legal limit. Depending on your plan's limits and your age, this could be $1,000 each month in 2002 (or approximately $1,600 per month in 2006). 401(k) also gives you the flexibility to adjust your contribution amount depending on your current circumstances and your changing retirement savings goals. Ideally, you will identify the savings rate necessary to achieve your retirement goals and stick with it over your working career. But if a change in your finances occurs, you could alter the amount you contribute to your 401(k) on a monthly basis.

Investment Flexibility

Your 401(k) plan allows you to select an investment mix that works for you. Typically, your 401(k) plan will offer you a wide variety of investment choices, allowing you to pick an aggressive, moderate, or conservative mix. 401(k) plans also allow you to change how your current account balance is allocated, as well as how your contributions are being allocated when they enter the plan. In most plans, you can initiate these changes whenever you want using Internet and voice response technology, and these changes may be made as quickly as the next day.

Preretirement Access

While the purpose of 401(k) plans is to help you prepare for retirement, they are structured so that you can take advantage of your 401(k) savings to address short-term emergencies. Plan loans allow you to borrow against your own funds. This access to your money helps you preserve your retirement savings while meeting immediate financial needs. In extreme cases, you can take out your funds via a hardship withdrawal. However, this is not recommended because the funds cannot be replaced.

Portability

You always own your 401(k) plan assets. If you change jobs or temporarily leave the work force, your money still belongs to you.

Even better, you have several options that keep your 401(k) money in a tax shelter—you can leave your assets in your former employer's plan, transfer them into an IRA, or transfer them into a new employer's plan. This is called *portability*. Portability permits you to keep your savings in a tax shelter, continue adding to your savings, and continue receiving the benefit of compounding.

It's Protected

Plan Security

Your 401(k) investments are protected. Your company employs plan trustees, administrators, and service providers—who may be fiduciaries. Fiduciaries have specific obligations under federal law to carefully manage your 401(k). Under the law, the assets in your plan are yours and must be managed solely for your benefit, never for the benefit of your employer or any other party. This means that the fiduciaries of your 401(k) plan are responsible for ensuring that every penny of your 401(k) money is where it is supposed to be.

The fiduciaries for your 401(k) are also held to a high standard of conduct under the law. A fiduciary who fails to follow the fiduciary responsibility rules is personally liable to the plan for all losses suffered as a result. In other words, if your plan managers mishandle your investments, they must pay you back out of their own pockets and return any money they made managing the funds.

One of the reasons that you know your company is doing everything it can to manage your 401(k) properly and keep your money safe is that those managing your company and the plan have their money in the 401(k) plan too!

Safe from Debt Collection

Your 401(k) money is always safe from debt collection. If you are very deeply in debt and must declare bankruptcy, most of your assets will be used to pay off your debts. Depending on the laws of your state, this could include your IRA. However, your 401(k) plan is protected from your creditors.

Also, if you have unpaid debts to individual companies, they may sue you in court for repayment. If you are sued, federal law protects 401(k) assets from any of the following pleas to the court:

- The removal of funds from your account, either by yourself or your plan administrator, to immediately pay your creditors
- The freezing of your 401(k) account until your debts are paid
- The earmarking of your assets to pay your debts when you remove your money years from now

Government Watchdogs

Not only must your company and your 401(k) plan fiduciaries follow federal law, they must also do so under the supervision of the government. The United States Department of Labor makes sure that your 401(k) assets are properly managed. The United States Treasury Department, along with the Internal Revenue Service, are responsible for ensuring that your company designs your plan correctly and administers it fairly for all employees.

Your company is required to file a report called a *Form 5500* with the government every year. Government agencies then review this report to make sure that your 401(k) plan is being properly managed. Government officials may also go to your company to evaluate the management of your 401(k) plan by conducting a special study called an *audit*. If your company or plan has breached its fiduciary obligations or committed a prohibited transaction, the government may fine the company and, more important to you, require that the company reimburse you for any losses you may have suffered.

The government and your employer do not guarantee investment returns. Rather, they protect plans and their participants by requiring that fiduciaries act responsibly and make plan benefits available on a nondiscriminatory basis.

Your Employer's Role

3

Employers set up 401(k) plans for three reasons: to attract, retain, and motivate high-quality workers like you. In order to accomplish this goal, employers design their 401(k) plans specifically for the employees at their company. This means that while the general principles of 401(k) participation are the same for all plans, the application of those principles may vary from company to company. Do not be surprised when you change jobs to find that your new 401(k) plan is different than your previous employer's plan.

The government encourages employers to offer 401(k) plans. Employer-provided benefit programs encouraged by the government—including 401(k)—are called *qualified plans*. This means that you and your employer are qualified to get the benefits of 401(k) plan participation only if your employer designs and operates your 401(k) plan within a framework of rules established by the government.

This chapter addresses your employer's role in setting up and maintaining your 401(k) plan. Government rules will be interwoven into the discussion as they apply. The chapter is divided into two sections:

1. Plan Design
2. Additional Support

To take full advantage of the opportunities your 401(k) provides, you must understand how your plan is designed and why. The Plan Design section outlines the choices your employer must consider when designing a 401(k) plan. For example, your employer makes important decisions about who can participate, whether or not to have matching contributions, the selection of investment choices, and more. Tips for getting the most from your company's specific 401(k) plan can be found in Chapter 4.

The Additional Support section describes other support that your employer performs for you and your 401(k) plan. This includes a discussion of the special 401(k) plan information provided to you by your employer, employer responsibility for monitoring your 401(k) investments, profit sharing, and employer compliance with federal law.

Plan Design

Employers have the flexibility to design a 401(k) plan tailored for their specific company and the needs of their employees. Within the 401(k) framework provided by the government, your employer is in charge of deciding:

- Who can participate in the plan
- When you are eligible to start contributing
- How much you can contribute to your plan
- Whether you must make investment choices or if the company will invest for you
- What your investment options are
- When and how often you can change your contribution amount or investment allocation
- Whether there will be an employer matching contribution and how much it will be
- When the matching contribution will be provided
- How long you have to work to earn the matching contribution (this is called *vesting*)
- Whether loans or hardship withdrawals will be permitted
- Whether to automatically enroll you in the plan
- Whether to accept rollovers from your IRA and/or other qualified plans

Who Can Participate

The right of an employee to save in a 401(k) plan is not automatic. However, full-time salaried and hourly employees are nearly always eligible to participate, and approximately half of companies sponsoring 401(k) plans allow their part-time employees to participate. On the other hand, many 401(k) plans exclude employees compensated on a commission basis, temporary employees, and leased employees. If you are a member of a union, your union contract may provide for 401(k) plan participation. In some cases, your 401(k) plan may include union members even if the union contract does not address 401(k) participation.

When You Can Start Saving

In order to start saving in your 401(k) plan, many companies require you to have at least one year of service with the company and be at least 21 years of age. Other companies let you start saving as soon as you start work or at the same time you are eligible for other company benefit programs, such as health coverage. Once you are eligible to participate you will probably have to wait for the next specific enrollment date to begin saving in your plan. This date could be the first of the month following your date of eligibility, which would allow for 12 enrollment dates every year; or your company might limit the enrollment dates to two a year, for example January 1st and July 1st.

If your company has a one-year eligibility requirement, in most cases your eligibility period is any 12-month period during which you were employed and you worked 1,000 hours. If you start out as a part-time worker ineligible for the plan, and then get hired to work full time, your part time employment must count towards your year of service.

Contribution Limits

Your employer wants to let you save in your 401(k) plan without limit, according to your own needs. However, your company must put a cap on what you can save to comply with contribution limits imposed by law and to provide for other payroll deductions.

There are two types of legal limits on employee 401(k) plan contributions: dollar limits and percentage limits. The amount that you can contribute is always the lower of any of these limits. The dollar denominated limit that employees can contribute to their 401(k) plans was $11,000 in 2002. This limit will increase by $1,000 every year until it reaches $15,000 in 2006. However, the ability to save the full dollar amount provided by law depends upon your meeting the percentage limitations as well.

Starting in 2002, your employer is permitted by law to let you save as much as 100 percent of your annual pay in your 401(k) plan. However, your employer cannot let you contribute so much to your 401(k) plan that there is no money left in your paycheck to pay your Social Security taxes or to make other payroll deductions, such as payment for your employer-provided health care plan. For this reason, companies allowing their employees to save more than 70 percent of their annual pay in a 401(k) plan are rare. But this is still a favorable percentage. If the percentage of pay allowed in your plan is 70 percent and your salary is $16,000 a year or more, you will be able to contribute $11,000 to your 401(k) plan in 2002— the full amount allowed by law. Note that many companies still limit the percentage of pay that employees may contribute to between 15 and 25 percent.

An additional percentage limitation may be imposed on employees that the law defines as "highly compensated." Basically, plans must maintain a legally set balance between the contributions of a company's highest-paid employees (in 2002, anyone earning $90,000 or more, or as indexed annually) and the contributions of other employees. If you fit the description of highly compensated, this means the percentage of your annual pay that you can contribute to your 401(k) plan may be limited. This will depend on the average contribution of those not defined as highly compensated. Your employer is responsible for determining this percentage limitation, communicating it to you, and making sure you do not exceed your limit.

Safe harbor contributions. Some plans provide a federally mandated match or contribution at a minimum level set by the federal government. This could be (1) either a 3 percent of pay employer contribution for all of eligible employees regardless of whether they are making 401(k) contributions themselves, or (2) a matching contribution of 100 percent on the first 3 percent of pay, and a 50 percent matching contribution on the next 2 percent of pay. Companies that adopt one of these contribution approaches are permitted to allow their highly-compensated employees to contribute the maximum amount provided by law without consideration of the average contribution of non-highly-compensated employees.

Catch-up contributions. Companies can allow employees 50 years of age or older to make additional contributions to their 401(k) plans. These contributions are not counted against any of the dollar or percentage limitations discussed previously, including the highly compensated percentage limitation. In fact, you must save the maximum possible (under your plan or the law) before you can make this additional contribution.

In 2002, this additional contribution can be as much as $1,000. The limit on this special contribution increases each year until 2006 when it will be $5,000. This means that beginning in 2006, those 50 years of age or older may be able to contribute $20,000 to their 401(k) plans ($15,000 plus a $5,000 catch-up contribution). It should be pointed out that this is a new provision in the law. Coordinating this special contribution with normal 401(k) plan limitations and company payroll systems is complex and some plans do not permit it, while others need time to comply with this feature.

Investment Process

How much money will you have in your 401(k) plan when you retire? Add together all of your contributions *and* the investment return on those contributions. If you have $100,000 in your account, a 6 percent annual return brings you $4,000 less than a 10 percent return. After 30 years of compounding, a 10 percent return is even more valuable. Because you want to get the best possible rate of return over your long-term time horizon, how your 401(k) money is invested is one of the most important plan design decisions.

Your employer always plays some part in your investment process, but when your 401(k) plan was first created your employer had to decide how much of a role it would play. Many plans are participant-directed, which means that you have the final say on asset allocation and investment. In some plans, you have control over the investment of your own contributions, but the company is responsible for investing the company contributions. In a few cases, the company is responsible for investing participant contributions as well.

Even if you make the final investment decision for all of your 401(k) funds, your company is still responsible for establishing a decision-making framework. This means that employers will pre-screen investment choices, providing a safer and less intimidating assortment of investment fund options. Typically, funds offered include a selection of equity and bond funds, plus a stable value fund or a money market fund. Please note that in some cases you may be asked to decide how your money will be invested before you are allowed to participate in your 401(k) plan. Some plans have a default option in the event you do not provide investment direction when you join the plan. You should find out what happens if no investment election is made.

In some 401(k) plans, if you want choices beyond those selected by your employer you may be permitted to invest directly in stocks, bonds, or mutual funds not offered by the plan. This investment alternative is often called a *brokerage window* or a *mutual fund window*. On the opposite end of the investment spectrum, 401(k) plans may also allow you to hand over your investment decisions to someone else. Companies do this by offering a professionally managed account (sometimes known as a lifestyle, lifecycle, or hybrid investment option) as an investment alternative. In a professionally managed account, your asset allocation decisions are made by investment professionals selected by your employer.

Contribution and Investment Allocation Flexibility

As a 401(k) participant, you have a great deal of control over your retirement program. You can decide when you want to contribute to your 401(k), how much to contribute, and where your money will be invested. So what role does your company play? In addition to selecting the investment options, your employer determines when and how often you can change your contribution and investment allocation. In some 401(k) plans, participants can change their asset allocation every day and the amount of their voluntary contribution every payroll period. Some plans only permit changes on a monthly or quarterly basis. Some plans let participants change as often as they like. Other plans permit only a limited number of changes. For example, a plan may permit participants to change their asset allocation whenever they want, but no more than eight times a year.

Matching Contributions

A 401(k) matching contribution is an employer contribution where the amount is based on how much you contribute to the plan. For example, in a plan with a dollar-for-dollar match up to 3 percent of pay, when you contribute 3 percent of your pay to the plan your employer will contribute the same amount. But if you do not contribute to the plan, neither will your employer.

Employers are not required to provide a match on your 401(k) contributions, but about 80 percent do. When a company is designing a 401(k) plan match program, it first decides the amount that will be matched and then decides how the company matching contribution will be determined. A company can choose from several different 401(k) matching approaches, the most common being a fixed match. A fixed match is based on a set percentage of the employee contribution. The most common fixed matching approach is an employer contribution of 50 cents for every dollar that the employee contributes, up to an employee contribution of 6 percent of pay.

Some companies have a graded match. This means that the percentage contributed by the company will vary depending upon the percentage of pay contributed by the participant. The most common graded match is a company contribution equal to 100 percent of the first 3 percent of pay contributed by the employee, and 50 percent of the next 2 percent of pay that the participant contributes.

A few companies base their 401(k) matching contribution on your years of service with the company. One company with this type of matching program matches up to 8 percent of pay based on the following schedule of service:

- 25 percent for those with one to five years of service
- 50 percent for those with six to ten years of service
- 75 percent for those with 11 to 15 years of service
- 100 percent for those with more than 15 years of service

Many employers tie the amount of their matching contribution to the company's financial success and profitability. As the profitability increases, the percentage contributed by the company increases as well. For example, when the company is having a really good year it contributes 100 percent of the first 6 percent that the employee contributes to the 401(k) plan, but when the company is having an average year it contributes 50 percent of the first 6 percent that the employee contributes. In a year in which the company is not profitable it would contribute nothing.

Timing of the match. Companies differ on when they contribute their matching dollars. Some match your money as soon as you contribute. Others put funds into your plan on a monthly, quarterly, or annual basis. Regardless of when your employer matches your 401(k) contribution, it means additional money building your account—money you didn't have to work for. An employer match is meant to encourage and reward you for participating in your company's plan, and it works.

Vesting

Employers do not want high-quality workers like you to quit, so they often design their 401(k) to reward employees who stay longer at the company. They do this by requiring employees to work several years at the company before they own the company contributions made to their 401(k) account. Even though your employer's contributions are deposited into your account, they are not yours until you have been at the company for a period of time determined by your employer. The money you contribute to the plan is always yours.

Vesting is the word used to describe how much of the company contributions, and the earnings on those company contributions, you own. If you have been at your company long enough to own part—but not all—of the employer contributions, you are said to be partially vested. When you own all of your company's contributions you are fully vested. Once you are fully vested, you are immediately vested for all future company contributions. You are always 100 percent vested in the money you contribute to a 401(k) plan.

There are three vesting approaches:

1. *Immediate vesting.* Some employers give you ownership of the company contributions at the time they are deposited in your account. A plan that does this is said to have immediate vesting.
2. *Graduated vesting.* In graduated vesting, the percentage of the employer contributions that you own increases over time until you reach 100 percent. (Federal law limits the maximum time this can take to up to six years.) For example, in two-year graduated vesting, you own 50 percent after the first year and all of the company contributions after the second year.
3. *Cliff vesting.* Some 401(k) plans have what is called cliff vesting, which provides full vesting after a certain length of service with no graduated vesting along the way. Employers using this method are required to give you full ownership of employer matching contributions no later than after three years of employment.

Each year that you work 1,000 hours is equal to one year on your vesting schedule. Similarly, if you have a month worth of vacation time stored up and you take it all at once, that time still counts toward your vesting schedule. If you take the vacation time in cash, however, the time may not be counted.

Loans and Hardship Withdrawals

Your employer decides whether your 401(k) plan will permit loans and hardship withdrawals and, if so, what rules will govern these provisions (within parameters set by federal law). Some employers feel that the availability of loans and hardship distributions from a 401(k) plan will reduce the ability of participants to save enough for their retirement. They are also concerned about the tax penalties that are imposed on preretirement distributions from a 401(k) plan.

Other employers believe that loans and hardship withdrawals are beneficial because they allow participants to have access to their money during emergencies. However, each plan has its own restrictions on the reasons for access to 401(k) plan savings and limitations on how much may be withdrawn. For detailed information on loans and hardship withdrawals, see Chapter 5.

Automatic Enrollment

Automatic enrollment is a practice by which your employer automatically enrolls you in your company's 401(k) plan once you become eligible, unless you actively decide not to participate. In automatic enrollment, your employer designates how much of your pay will be contributed and how it will be invested. According to federal law, companies can automatically enroll their participants in their 401(k) plans as long as they:

- Give adequate notice of enrollment at a reasonable period before the enrollment date
- Provide the right to change the contribution amount

If your plan has automatic enrollment and you do not wish to participate, your notice of enrollment form will give you the option not to join the plan. You must complete the necessary forms (usually just a a box to check) and turn it in to your plan administrator as soon as possible. Because you are reading this book, I will assume that you welcome the idea of 401(k) plan participation.

Automatic enrollment moves a specific percentage of your pay into the plan every pay period, most often 3 percent, where it is invested for you. The approach to investing automatic contributions varies from company to company. Some companies invest the money in stable value or mutual funds, others put the money into a balanced fund or a professionally managed account. However, this is your money and you generally have the right to make your own investment decisions. The forms required to change your investment options should also be included in your notice of enrollment materials.

Why do employers and employees value this practice? Many employees believe that they don't know how to invest or don't make enough money to even bother saving. When employees see their assets growing it gets their attention and teaches them the value of retirement savings. The only drawback to automatic enrollment is that some employees never change their contribution rate, staying at that low, introductory 3 percent rate. This provides a benefit, but not as much as contributing at a more appropriate, higher level.

Rollovers into the Plan

If you have a new job, you might want to put the 401(k) money you accumulated at your previous employer into your new employer's 401(k) plan. Also, you might want to put your IRA money or your other qualified retirement plan distributions, if you have any, in your new employer's 401(k) plan. Many companies design their 401(k) plans to accept such rollovers. Those that do not accept rollovers from non-401(k) retirement programs are unable to handle the administrative complexity that accepting such rollovers requires. In this case, you may roll your distribution over into an IRA.

Other Employer Support

Employer-Provided Information

Your employer regularly provides you with information about your 401(k) plan. In its communications with you, your company will:

- Explain your plan and how to use it
- Explain your rights under the law
- Provide you with investment information

This information is so important that you should keep everything you receive even if it is not given to you on paper. If your employer sends you information by e-mail, keep a copy of the e-mail and save it with other plan-related documents.

Summary plan description. The most important document you will receive about your 401(k) plan is called a *summary plan description* (SPD). The SPD is a government-required communication that includes:

- General information about the plan (i.e., the name of the plan, the plan sponsor, and the plan administrator)
- The plan's eligibility requirements
- A summary of the plan's benefits
- Plan contributions and other funding information
- The plan's claims procedure
- An explanation of your legal rights

All the issues we've mentioned in this chapter (eligibility, vesting, matching contributions) plus those discussed in other chapters (loans, hardship withdrawals, distributions, and more) are covered in the SPD. Additionally, this document provides information on the appeals process should you have problems with the management of your plan.

You should receive a copy of your 401(k) plan's SPD when you join the plan, or shortly thereafter. Your plan's SPD is also available anytime upon request. If you do not currently have yours, contact your human resources department and ask for a copy. Keep your SPD in a safe place so you can refer to it whenever you have a question. The entire framework of your 401(k) plan is contained within the SPD. Use it well.

Other plan documents. Your employer will also provide other explanatory materials, for example, your plan balance statement. This information, typically sent out quarterly, includes your contributions, your employer's contributions, the amount of money in your account, the status of your various investments, the distribution of your asset allocation, any changes you made to your account during the period, and any loans or withdrawals.

In addition, your plan has probably provided you with written information to help you invest your 401(k) plan assets. These materials are designed to help you make good asset allocation and investment decisions. Typically, they will be tailored for the actual investment options offered by your 401(k) plan. These and any other documents you receive from your employer are important reference materials and should be kept on file. Your employer may also provide investment education tools, such as newsletters, education or advice via the Internet, or financial planning assistance.

Managing Plan Investments

Federal law imposes a high level of responsibility on employers who offer 401(k) plans. According to the law, your employer is a fiduciary responsible for managing your 401(k) plan assets according to the "prudent man" standard. This requires a 401(k) plan fiduciary to act with care, skill, prudence, and diligence. However, fiduciaries are not required to be experts in every area. They can and often do hire outside advisors, such as attorneys, accountants, administrators, and investment managers. Fiduciaries are required to choose quality managers and monitor their performance.

A fiduciary is also expected to have control of the plan assets. This means that a fiduciary is responsible for making sure that your money is where it is supposed to be when it is supposed to be there. As a fiduciary, your employer is also responsible for ensuring that your payroll savings are deposited into your 401(k) account in a timely manner, and that the 401(k) plan is administered for the exclusive benefit of its participants and their beneficiaries.

These special requirements are some of the reasons for the uniformly high quality of plan administration and oversight throughout the 401(k) system. They provide you with a level of safety within your employer-offered 401(k) plan that you probably would not have if you invested on your own. However, the prudent man standard does not guarantee investment performance.

Profit Sharing

The most popular plan offered today combines profit sharing with a 401(k) plan. This approach offers all the advantages of 401(k) with an extra incentive—an employer-provided contribution based on the financial success of the company. Companies that offer a profit sharing contribution in addition to the 401(k) feature generally have greater company contributions than those with only a fixed match. As a result, your account balance will grow more quickly and it will be easier to achieve your retirement goals.

There are many different approaches to profit sharing. For example, the amount and timing of profit sharing contributions are based upon the specifications of the sponsoring company. More than half of profit sharing/401(k) plans base a portion of their company's contribution on overall profits, tying retirement success to personal productivity and company success. In such cases, the profit sharing bonus is contributed as a lump sum at the end of each year, after the company's success has been determined. In other profit sharing/401(k) plans, the company contribution is made in company stock rather than in cash. This approach will be discussed more in Chapter 9.

Profit sharing contributions to a 401(k) plan should not be confused with cash profit sharing that is added directly to your paycheck at regular intervals (annually being the most common). Sometimes your employer will give you the option of contributing part of your cash profit sharing as a 401(k) contribution. This may be described as "cash or deferred" election.

Legal Compliance

Your employer is required to administer your 401(k) according to rules established by the government. Complying with these rules is quite complicated and requires a significant effort by your employer, and your employer takes these rules quite seriously. Failure to comply with the rules could have severe consequences as the plan could be disqualified, in which case all of your contributions and plan earnings would be made immediately taxable and your employer would lose tax deductions taken from the contributions. These rules are intended to ensure that your 401(k) plan is designed and managed for the benefit of all of its participants. For example, these rules make sure that there is broad plan participation with no special treatment for company executives. In fact, some of these rules restrict the contributions of company executives and other highly compensated employees more than those of lower-compensated participants.

4

Make the Most of
Your Company's Plan

Companies—be they technology corporations, manufacturing plants, or attorney offices—are all distinctly different. Each company's 401(k) plan has been designed to meet the specific needs of that company and its unique work force. Your plan may be designed to have a generous employer matching contribution, it may have a small match but include a profit sharing contribution option, or it may have no match but offer a defined benefit plan as well as a 401(k).

Other differences in plans include the time it takes for you to own the money contributed in your account by your employer (called vesting), or the number and types of investment options offered by your employer. The key is to know your particular plan so you can make it work for you. This chapter suggests some fundamental ways you can make the most of your company's plan.

This chapter is the first of several chapters that will help you take full advantage of your 401(k) plan's many opportunities. Chapter 5, "When You Need Your Money Now," describes the types of pre-retirement distributions, including loans and hardship withdrawals, that you may be able to take from your account. Asset allocation and investment choices are covered in detail in Chapters 6, 9, and 10, which focus on all aspects of 401(k) investing. 401(k) plans that offer the employer's stock as an investment are discussed in Chapter 8. Managing your 401(k) in a job transition is the topic of Chapter 12.

Participation

Everyone knows that participation is the basic element in making your 401(k) plan work for you. However, many don't realize that knowing if you can participate in your employer's plan is just as critical. Do not assume when you start a new job that you do not meet the requirements for 401(k) plan participation simply because you are new to the company or work part-time. Ask your employer when you start your new position. Do not wait to be told. If you want to make the most of your company's plan, you need to take responsibility for knowing how it works. That starts with knowing if and when you can participate.

Start Saving Now

In a 401(k) plan, your money starts to grow the instant you contribute to the plan. So make the most of your plan and join as soon as possible! Different companies have different starting dates. Find out when you can start saving, complete your enrollment forms and return them right away. It is easy to procrastinate and suddenly find your initial eligibility date has passed. Getting your paperwork in early means that you will start saving as soon as you are eligible to participate.

Also, if you are eligible to join your plan a year down the line, don't depend on your employer to remind you when it is time to participate. Mark your calendar, then be sure to complete your enrollment forms and turn them in on time, or ahead of time, if allowed.

Get That Company Match

Some companies make matching employer contributions to their 401(k) plans. Typically, an employer match is a percentage of what you contribute to the plan up to a maximum amount—for example, 50 cents for every dollar up to 6 percent of your salary. Employers provide this as an incentive to you to save for retirement. It doesn't matter if your company's match is a generous $1 for $1 contribution or just a few pennies. A company match is a risk-free addition to your savings that requires no work and is not taxed as income. In other words, this is free money, so don't pass it up!

Likewise, be sure you get the entire match. If your employer matches up to 6 percent of pay, make sure you contribute 6 percent of pay. If your employer matches up to 10 percent of pay, meet that amount. Even if it means cutting back on your gourmet coffee and daily muffin, contribute enough to your 401(k) to get the full company match. Remember, what you contribute now will be worth many times more to you later.

Companies do not determine their matching contributions in the same way or contribute their match at the same time. Some contribute the company match when they deposit your own contribution into the plan, which may be as frequently as every pay period. Others contribute the match after a period of time, typically on an annual basis. It is important to be aware of the timing of your company's match. This will ensure that you know what to expect and can contribute in a way that will maximize your employer's matching contribution.

If your plan provides the match at the end of the year, you can contribute different amounts throughout the year and still receive the full match. But you must be aware of other rules. For example, if you leave the company before the day of the match—even one day before the match will be put into the plan—you may not receive the matching contribution. If you decide to change jobs, you should consider the timing of the employer matching contribution when you pick your termination date.

Different rules apply at companies that match at the same time your own contributions are deposited. For example, if you must contribute 6 percent of your pay to get the full match, you may have to contribute 6 percent of each paycheck you receive during the year. This means if you want to reduce your contributions for half of the year then make up the difference with large contributions for the rest of the year, you may not receive the full match. Some companies do go back and calculate the total contributed at the end of the plan year and make an additional matching contribution. The key is to know what your plan will allow.

Start Early

What you save earlier in your career earns longer. This reduces how much you may have to save later. Someone who saves consistently for 11 years between ages 24 and 35, and then stops saving but keeps the money invested until retirement, will have approximately as much money as someone who waits until age 35 to start saving and then saves for 30 years.

For example, Pat is making $25,000 at age 24 when he begins participating in his company's 401(k). He contributes 6 percent of pay and the company makes a 50 percent match on that amount. If Pat gets an 8 percent rate of return and receives salary increases of 2.5 percent every year, he will have $43,345 in his account when he is 35. He stops contributing at that time but keeps his money in his 401(k), where he earns an 8 percent return on that money, when he is 65, he will have $436,165 without having made another contribution for 30 years.

Gerry, on the other hand, does not start saving until she is 35. At age 24 she was making the same as Pat ($25,000), and at her current age she is making $32,800, thanks to a 2.5 percent salary increase every year. Like Pat, Gerry now contributes 6 percent of pay, and the company matches 50 percent of that amount. Also, Gerry earns an 8 percent rate of return and continues to receive the 2.5 percent salary increase. When she retires at age 65 after 30 years of contributions and earnings, she will have $444,279, only $8,114 more than Pat. Pat will have contributed less than $20,000, while Gerry will have contributed nearly four times as much to reach the same amount. Of course, you can be smarter than both Pat and Gerry by starting early and consistently saving in your 401(k) year after year.

Maximize Your Contribution

Can you imagine complaining that you have *too much* saved for retirement? Making the most of your 401(k) plan means contributing the most that you can when you can. Why set your contribution level low? Find out what the maximum contribution for your plan is. Then save as close to the maximum as you can. You may not always be able to save as much as you can now and it is good to get ahead.

The beauty of a higher contribution level is that you can always cut back in the future. You may be able to easily change your contribution rate on a quarterly, monthly, or even daily basis, depending on your plan. Perhaps for one year you can contribute the maximum, while for another you may only be able to put the minimum into your plan.

You can also stop contributing entirely at any time, but find how your plan works before you do. In some cases, if you choose to quit saving completely you may be locked out of contributing to your plan for an entire year. Remember, your tax benefit is not just about a future date when you retire—your tax savings begin the day you begin to participate in your plan. Any money you contribute to your plan not only postpones your taxes, it can often lower your tax bracket as well, reducing your overall income tax rate.

If you cannot make the maximum contribution right away, gradually increase your 401(k) contribution over time. For example, if initially you can only save 5 percent of your pay, increase the amount you save by 1 percent of pay each time you get a raise. Sooner than you know it, you will be at your plan's maximum.

Once you have set your contribution at your plan's maximum amount, the payroll deductions become automatic. You will most likely adjust to that level of income and never think about it again, all the while reaping the benefit of those tax-free dollars going straight into your account. However, make sure to increase your contribution amount every year to meet the contribution limit increases provided by law. When you reach the age of 50, remember to make additional catch-up contributions over the legal limit, if they are allowed in your plan.

Another opportunity for maximizing the value of your contribution is the low-income and moderate-income saver credit on your income tax, described in detail in Chapter 2. If you are eligible, this credit provides as much as 50 percent back on a contribution of up to $2,000, or a credit of $1,000 on your income taxes. If your company match provides 50 cents on the dollar for your contribution and the saver's credit provides 50 cents on the dollar as well, your entire contribution has been repaid.

If you are seeking to contribute the absolute maximum amount possible, some plans allow additional after-tax contributions. This money will not reduce your taxable income now, but at the end of the road when you withdraw your funds for retirement, you will not have to pay taxes on these after-tax contributions. Any earnings on after-tax contribution investment will not be taxed until you with-draw them from the plan.

Vesting

Your 401(k) plan's vesting schedule defines how much of your company's contributions, and the earnings on those contributions, you own. Usually, this depends on how long you have worked for the company. No matter what vesting approach your employer uses, if you leave your company before you are 100 percent vested, you will be leaving without all of the company contributions. If you intend to stay at your current employer for just a few years, make sure you know your plan's vesting schedule and try to time your termination to maximize your ownership of the company's contributions.

Automatic Enrollment

Your company may have enrolled you in its 401(k) plan auto-matically. This means that part of your earnings are automatically withheld from each of your paychecks and deposited in the 401(k) plan, until you tell the company to stop. If you have been auto-matically enrolled in your company's 401(k) plan, you should un-derstand that the amount of your pay being withheld is not likely to be enough to provide you with what you will need in retirement. The amount being withheld is a minimum amount that your em-ployer has decided will get you started down the path of retire-ment saving. Also, the way your 401(k) money is invested in an automatic enrollment arrangement may not be right for you. Check the investment allocation on your participant statement.

If you are participating in your plan by automatic enrollment, consider your current contribution rate and your employer pro-vided investments. If you can, start saving more and reallocate your plan investments to meet your special goals. If you cannot save a lot more all at once, consider increasing your contribution by 1 percent every year until you at least reach the percentage necessary to get the full employer matching contribution. Whatever you decide to do, make sure you make choices that are right for you.

Employer-Provided Information

In Chapter 3, we discussed some of the information provided by your employer, including your summary plan description (SPD) and your account balance statement. Save every communication you receive in a three-ring binder, as you will definitely need to refer to these documents throughout your working career.

Managing the Paperwork

There's nothing more annoying than forms to fill out, especially if you already handle administrative duties in your job. But I cannot stress this enough: Pay close attention to the details of your company's 401(k) plan. Following directions, signing your documents, and filing your forms on time means more money later. In a 401(k) plan, any delays will prevent you from contributing the maximum amount and reaching the maximum benefit. Perhaps you put off completing the necessary forms because it is too confusing or intimidating. Never fear! You can always call your plan's customer service number to ask for help and explanations.

Naming Your Beneficiary

It is your beneficiary designation form, not your will, that determines who will inherit the funds from your 401(k) plan, your IRA, and other retirement accounts. The assets still in these accounts will pass directly to your beneficiary without going through probate as long as you fill out the paperwork. If you do not name a beneficiary or if the beneficiary named in your plan is not your current beneficiary, your assets could go through probate after your death. This means that high attorney fees and court costs could eat away your funds. It might also allow creditors access to your money before your family.

To be sure that your money goes to whom you want, be sure to name a beneficiary and a contingent beneficiary on your beneficiary form. Your contingent beneficiary is the person who would inherit your account if your primary beneficiary passes away before you or at the same time. If you want to name someone other than your spouse (e.g. a trust or one of your children), your spouse must consent to your beneficiary election and your spouse's signature must be notarized. Also, remember to review and/or change your beneficiary form when you get married or divorced, or when there is a death in your family. Keep a record of these designations filed with other important papers so you (or others) can find the information when it is needed.

Spousal Consent

If you are married, your plan may require that your spouse sign documents for loans, hardship withdrawals, distributions at retirement, or other aspects of your plan that involve the movement of money. Know your plan requirements before you decide to make decisions that affect distribution of your plan assets.

Educational Materials

In this age of investment options and asset allocation, your company most likely offers many educational resources. These will cover the basic concepts of investment, your plan's investment options, and how to make responsible 401(k) decisions, but they also may explain recent changes in your plan and the latest legislative developments. Nearly all plans provide printed educational materials, but your employer may also be posting educational information about your plan on the Internet or its own intranet, providing modeling software, or showing educational videotapes. Don't let these valuable (and free) resources go untapped!

Using Technology

Technology advances have permitted increasing 401(k) plan flexibility *and* lowered the cost of administration. Consider the staff that would have been necessary to administer just one of today's large 401(k) plans if we were limited to the resources of the 1980s. The Roman Coliseum would not be large enough to house all of the accounting clerks.

You have a number of technology options to help you understand and manage your plan. Make sure you take advantage of these options whenever possible. With a minimum of hassle, and 24 hour-a-day access, these systems generally allow you to:

- Enroll in your plan
- Change your contribution rate
- Inquire about your plan balance
- Change your investments
- Obtain a plan loan
- Request a hardship distribution
- Plan for your retirement future

In any system that does not involve human interaction, you will access your account with PIN numbers and passwords. Write down your access codes and store them in a secure place or memorize them to ensure that your account remains secure. Do not share them with others.

Telephone Systems

Automated telephone systems are currently the standard technology method for employee access to individual accounts. They are available in more than 80 percent of plans. Typically, participants can use an automated telephone system for balance inquiries, loan requests, and changes to investments and contributions. Increasingly, these systems recognize spoken language in addition to input through the keypad.

Most companies have telephone-accessed staffed service centers, typically contacted through an 800 number. These centers provide 401(k) participants with live people who can answer participant questions and help with plan transactions. Companies are most likely to use telephone accessed service centers to assist participants in their initial enrollment or with arranging final distributions.

Computer Systems

Internet-accessed support for 401(k) plan participants is nearly as common as automated telephone systems. As technology-assisted practices grow more prevalent, nearly all companies will give their employees access to their 401(k) accounts over the Internet.

Intranet systems, or computerized systems for use only within the sponsoring company, are uncommon except at very large employers. They provide 401(k) participants with all of the services of an Internet-based system with the added security that access is available only through the company.

New Technologies

In addition to telephone and computer-accessed systems, the latest technology innovations—for example, data aggregation, account consolidation, e-servicing, and holistic investment advice—are providing valuable opportunities for 401(k) participants. However, technologies continue to change rapidly, public policy is uncertain, and possible fiduciary consequences have not been totally assessed. Before you rush to use every new technology available, make sure you consider how safe and secure those systems are.

Also, be careful if you intend to access your 401(k) account using an Internet entry other than the one provided by your employer or your employer's selected 401(k) plan administrator. Some Web site companies engage in activities that could infringe on your privacy. These activities include both hidden tracking through unauthorized programs called *cookies,* and the misuse of information when data about Web site users is sold to others for cross-selling. Be sure to read each Web site's privacy statement to know how that site will protect your privacy rights. Web sites without a privacy statement should be avoided.

Profit Sharing

Profit sharing ties the collective effort of employees to the company's financial success. One type of profit sharing rewards employees with contributions to their retirement plan. Some companies with fixed 401(k) matches make profit sharing contributions to the accounts of all employees, even those who have not contributed to the 401(k) plan. Other profit sharing companies base all or part of their 401(k) matching contributions upon the company's current profitability. These matches will be higher than average in good years and lower when the company is unprofitable. Some companies have no 401(k) matching contributions but make profit sharing contributions for all their employees. Profit sharing companies typically make larger contributions overall to their plans than other companies.

If you are fortunate enough to have both profit sharing and 401(k), it is even more important that you know how your plan works. You need to consider the total company contribution in your retirement savings decision. You need to know when you are eligible to receive the profit sharing bonus because typically only those employed on the last day of the company fiscal year are eligible. You need to review the vesting rules as some companies have different vesting schedules for the 401(k) match and the profit sharing contribution.

Coordinate with Your Spouse

Being married should affect your 401(k) decision making. If your spouse does not have a 401(k) plan at work, or is not currently part of the work force, you are saving for your combined retirement needs. If this is the case, your contribution amount should reflect a target goal that supports you both after you stop working.

Do not underestimate and save for just one; in retirement, you will be faced with grocery bills, housing, and health costs for two.

Perhaps both you and your spouse work for companies that offer 401(k) plans. First, your combined savings rates should build sufficient assets to support both of you in retirement. Second, you want to divide your contributions to get the full matching contribution in both plans. If you cannot save enough to get both matches, your priority should first be saving in the plan with the richest match, and then in the plan with the best vesting schedule. Finally, you want to concentrate your additional contributions in the plan with the best investment options and the best plan loan program or other preretirement access to your 401(k) plan assets.

Let's say that Pat and Gerry are married, each with the option to participate in a different plan. Both earn a salary of $50,000, and can expect a 2.5 percent increase in pay every year. Pat's 401(k) plan provides a company match of 50 cents for every dollar he contributes up to 6 percent of pay, while Gerry's plan has no match. They would like to save $3,000 a year for 30 years between the two plans. What is their best option? If they split the money evenly between the two plans, assuming an 8 percent return from both, their end result will be $560,035 ($336,021 from Pat's plan and $224,014 from Gerry's). But if they save entirely in Pat's plan they will net a total of $672,042. That's $112,000 more without any additional contributions, time, or hassle. Figure 4.1 illustrates these two options.

The fact that marital status has an effect on 401(k) plan decision making illustrates the broader principle that your 401(k) plan is just one part of your overall financial picture. This means that 401(k) choices should not be made in isolation. 401(k) decision making should include consideration of your complete financial and personal situation.

FIGURE 4.1   Spouses Should Choose the Better Plan in Which to Save

Assumptions: *Gerry's plan—no match*
Pat's plan—50 cent match up to 6 percent of pay
Starting salary—$50,000 year each   *Contribution—3 percent of pay each*
Time span—30 years   *Rate of return—8 percent*
Salary increase—2.5 percent per year

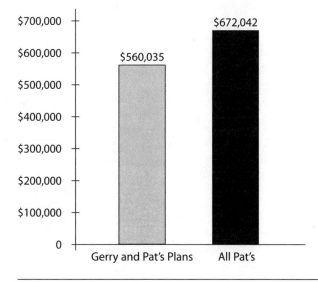

5

When You Need
Your Money Now

Ideally, you will never touch your retirement funds, allowing them to grow continuously for retirement. But we don't live in an ideal world! In case of emergency, your funds may be available to you in the form of loans and hardship withdrawals. If you become disabled or pass away, you or your beneficiary can immediately have access to your account. If you retire early, you may also take an early distribution. If you are considering taking money from your plan before you retire, please read this chapter closely to understand the options available to you.

Loans

One of the benefits offered by most 401(k) plans is the ability to borrow against your retirement savings in times of need. Currently, about 20 percent of employees eligible for a plan loan have taken advantage of the option, with an average outstanding loan balance of about $6,300.

Loans provide two special advantages:

1. If your plan has a loan program, you have the security of knowing that your money is available "just in case." This means you can comfortably make the maximum contribution commitment to your plan without worrying if you might need those funds later.
2. Loans help prevent you from depleting your retirement savings when financial crisis occurs. If your plan offers loans,

you will be required to take a loan first before you can take a distribution because once money is taken as a distribution, it cannot be replaced.

Let's assume you have an unexpected crisis and you need your money. What should you know?

Loan Basics

- Plans typically allow you to borrow up to 50 percent of your vested plan assets, up to $50,000, less the amount of any outstanding plan loans.
- Plan loans usually have a minimum amount requirement, which is typically $1,000.
- Loans may be taken from all vested funds, which includes your rollovers from other qualified plans.
- In nearly all cases, you must repay your loan in equal payments over a five-year period.
- In rare cases, your payment period may be longer when the loan is for your primary residence.
- The interest rate you pay will be set on the day you take the loan. While rates vary by plan, prime rate plus 1 percent is most common. Contact your plan administrator to find out what your loan rate will be.
- Almost all plans use payroll deduction for repayment of your loan. Other methods of repayment are rare.
- You can repay your loan in full at any time.
- Many plans allow more than one plan loan.

Pros and Cons

Plan loans are convenient, but they aren't always the right solution. Consider both the positives and negatives to determine if a plan loan is best for you, and always compare the overall cost of a plan loan with other possible loans.

Plan loan advantages:

- *Less paperwork.* There are no credit checks or long credit application forms. You may be able to get a plan loan by simply visiting your benefits office, calling your plan's 800 number, or going online.
- *No restrictions.* Most plans let you borrow for any reason. Check your plan.
- *Fast.* You could receive a loan in mere days, depending on how often your plan processes transactions.
- *Good rates.* Prime rate plus 1 percent is the interest rate banks charge their best customers. This is a very good rate of interest for an individual borrower.
- *Higher return.* The rate of repayment for your loan may be greater than the rate of return you were receiving on your fixed investment. If you replace assets from your money market fund (paying 4 percent) with your plan loan (paying 7 percent) you would be earning a higher rate of return.

Plan loan disadvantages:

- *Loan default.* Failure to repay counts as a hardship withdrawal, which means your money is taxed and you must pay a 10 percent early withdrawal federal income tax penalty on the outstanding balance if you are under age 59$\frac{1}{2}$.
- *Fees.* Seventy percent of plans charge a one-time loan fee, ranging from $3 to $100. Another 25 percent of plans also charge a yearly service fee, from $3 to $75.
- *Alters financial plan.* You've done the work to determine your retirement goal and pick the right investment mix. But when you take a plan loan, money must be removed from your plan investments. If the loan must be taken from your equity investments, this may diminish your overall plan return.
- *Market cost.* Cash for your loan may come from selling shares from mutual funds or stocks. If you sell when the market is down and take a loss, you will reduce your long-term investment return.

- *Lower return.* The rate of repayment for your loan may be lower than the rate of return you were receiving on your fixed investment. If you replace assets from your diversified equity fund (paying 10 percent) with your plan loan (paying 7 percent) you would be earning a lower rate of return.
- *Spousal consent.* You may need to get your spouse's permission for a loan.

How Loans Work

There is a popular misconception that paying back a plan loan is like paying yourself. Unfortunately, this is not true. When you take a loan from your plan, you are withdrawing money from your account balance and replacing it with an IOU. That IOU continues to generate interest from your repayments, but generates no investment return. Also, money to pay back a loan is double taxed— first when you make the payment and again when you receive the distribution from your account. From an investment point of view, it is far better not to take a loan and continue to generate a tax-deferred return from your investment.

In a sense, all investments are a kind of loan. You are lending money to the government or to a corporation through the stable value, money market, or bond funds in your plan. However, the return (or interest) generated from *these* loans comes from the borrowing party. When you loan yourself the money you are simply replacing the return you would already be receiving with interest payments from yourself.

Plan Loans and Your Investments

To preserve your asset allocation when taking a plan loan, you should withdraw the funds for a loan from the fixed income allocation side of your portfolio or the lowest returning investment option. Let's assume you have 50 percent of your money invested in stock, also known as equities, and 50 percent invested in fixed income. When you borrow 50 percent of the money in your plan, you want to take the funds entirely from the fixed income side and maintain all the equities. Some plans will ask you to make that decision, others will reduce all of your investments proportionally by the amount of your plan loan. In that event, you need to go back and rebalance the remaining investments to the proper equity and fixed allocation ratios.

Warning: Don't Default on Your Loan

This is crucial: If you leave your current employer, have no outstanding plan loans. Whether you find a new position or you are laid off, in most cases, your plan loan will come due when employment ends. You will be given a limited amount of time to pay off your loan, and if you cannot repay it will be placed in default. If you take a loan, be sure you understand the repayment requirements in case you terminate employment.

"In default" means your employer will report to the government that you were unable to pay the loan, and the government will then treat the defaulted amount of your loan as a hardship distribution. This will lead to regular taxes on the defaulted amount plus the 10 percent hardship withdrawal penalty if you are younger than age $59\frac{1}{2}$. Depending on your tax bracket and the tax rate of your state, you could be penalized by as much as half of the defaulted amount. Some people will take a cash advance on their credit card to pay off the plan loan, because the 18 percent interest on the credit amount is still better than a 50 percent tax liability.

Hardship Withdrawals

Plans that permit hardship withdrawals during employment do so for specific purposes identified in your plan. Typically, these include:

- *Medical.* These costs include medical expenses for you, your spouse, or any dependents. Medical expenses that are deductible for income tax purposes are not subject to the additional 10 percent penalty on preretirement distributions.

- *Education.* You can withdraw money for post–high school expenses for the next 12 months. These costs include tuition, room and board, books, and other related expenses.
- *Principal residence.* A withdrawal may be taken to use as a down payment on your principal home. Mortgage payments or secondary residences are not included. However, withdrawals are permitted to prevent eviction from your residence or foreclosure on your home.

The decision to take a hardship withdrawal from your plan is a serious one. Please keep in mind the following:

- A hardship withdrawal is not a loan. Once taken out, these funds cannot be replaced.
- If you take a hardship withdrawal before age $59\frac{1}{2}$, a 10 percent early withdrawal federal income tax penalty will be imposed, in addition to regular taxes on the amount withdrawn.
- Tax with be withheld on any money you withdraw. By law, your plan will deduct and pay to the federal government a percentage of the money you withdraw. At tax time, you will likely owe additional taxes in addition to those withheld.
- If you take a hardship withdrawal, you may be prohibited from making contributions to your plan for a period of time, thus losing the opportunity to save pretax money or receive your employer's match during that time.

Hardship withdrawals come with serious penalties to discourage you from taking money out. Your hardship has to be pretty hard to make it worth all this trouble. When your financial problem is that serious, you must also determine if it meets the hardship specifications.

Early Distribution

In several situations there may be an early distribution from your plan. This is good because you do not have to wait; but it can come with a heavy cost. As you know, when you receive a distribution you must report that money as income and pay taxes on it. But if you take a distribution before the age 59½ you may also have to pay an additional 10 percent early withdrawal federal income tax penalty, which can seriously reduce your retirement funds. The key is to know how to avoid this extra tax.

The government provides several possible ways for you to sidestep the 10 percent early withdrawal federal income tax penalty when you retire. However, the IRS has strict rules, so dot your *i*'s and cross your *t*'s.

Age 55 Early Retirement

The concept of an early retirement is seductive. Who wouldn't want to retire in their early 50s and enjoy the good life? The government recognizes this attraction and offers you a compromise— simply stay at your current employer until the year you turn 55, then retire. Notice that you don't have to be exactly 55. You can retire on January 1 of the calendar year in which you will eventually become 55. Also, you don't have to stay retired. You can go to work again, even for the same employer. But to receive the age 55 distribution, you must at some point terminate your employment and retire.

If you are thinking of retiring at age 53 and keeping the money in your plan two more years, think again. Just keeping your money in the plan until age 55 will not prevent an early distribution tax. You must actually continue employment until the year you turn 55.

Periodic Payments

Both the IRS and some plans permit you to take regular payments from your account over time. These payments will be taxed as ordinary income but will not receive the 10 percent early withdrawal federal income tax penalty, regardless of your age.

However, there are two requirements. First, you must have terminated employment before payments begin. Second, you must conform to the IRS required format and computation method for determining payments. The IRS only provides for "substantially equal" fixed payments, based on the life expectancy of you and your spouse.

Qualified Domestic Relations Order (QDRO) Payments

Your plan can be forced to distribute your plan assets to pay child support, alimony, or a settlement to a former spouse as required by a QDRO. Such distributions will be taxed as income but will not receive the additional 10 percent early withdrawal penalty. However, a valid QDRO that clearly defines how the account is to be shared must be in place, not just an informal agreement.

If you are planning to get a divorce, make sure your attorney contacts the plan administrator before the divorce is final to determine the plan's requirements for a QDRO. Many plans have sample QDROs that will assist your divorce attorney with this process.

Disability

If you become permanently disabled you can withdraw money from your plan. Such distributions are taxed as income but are free from the 10 percent early withdrawal federal income tax penalty. However, the IRS is particular about who they deem disabled. In order to be considered disabled, the law requires that you be unable to engage in any substantial gainful activity. You must be able to prove both the existence and the permanence of the disability, with an emphasis on how this condition is unchangeable, to be allowed access to your funds.

Death

If you die, your beneficiary will receive the money in your 401(k) account. If you do not designate a beneficiary, the money will go to your spouse automatically. However, the money will go to your spouse regardless of who you designate as your beneficiary unless your spouse has agreed in advance to an alternate agreement. Your spouse will be required to pay regular income taxes on these funds, but the 10 percent early withdrawal federal income tax penalty will not apply. Spouses may also roll the money over tax-free into their own IRA or employer-provided plan, deferring taxes until they withdraw the money. Please note that if your account balance is more than $5,000, your spouse (but not other beneficiaries) may keep the money in the plan until the date you would have reached age 70$\frac{1}{2}$.

6

401(k) Investing
The Basics

401(k) money management is critical to your long-term financial security. For participants, the return on their investments could be several times the amount they save. This is the first of six chapters that address 401(k) investing. Chapters 6, 7, and 8 will discuss the investments that are most frequently offered in a 401(k) plan. Chapters 9 and 10 will address how 401(k) assets should be managed. Chapter 11 is devoted to helping you develop your own 401(k) investment plan.

In most 401(k) plans, your employer will offer you a range of investment funds from which to choose. Some 401(k) plans also offer other types of options, like a brokerage window, a mutual fund window, or a professionally managed account. This chapter will discuss the types of investments that are likely to be found in a 401(k) plan. Two investment options that are special to 401(k) plans and other defined-contribution retirement programs, stable value funds and employer stock, are discussed separately in Chapters 7 and 8.

Three Main Types of Investments

Generally, three types of assets make up the investment funds in a 401(k) plan: stocks, bonds, and cash. Each of these has different traits, such as rate of return, purpose, and appropriate time span for investment.

Stocks

- Average rate of return: Approximately 10 percent
- Purpose: Growth
- Time span: Long term, typically ten years or more

If you own a company's stock, you are a part owner in that company. Because you are a part owner, you have a piece or share of the equity in that company. That is why stocks are also called *equities*. If the company has 100 shares of stock and you own one share, you own 1/100 of the company. The value of a share of stock is the total market value of the company divided by the number of shares. The stocks of public companies are traded on a stock exchange and you can look up their value in your daily newspaper. The stock of a privately held company is owned by an individual or small group and is not actively traded.

Stocks generate return in two ways. First, successful companies increase in value. This means that the value of the stock also increases, increasing the wealth of stockholders. Second, some companies pay some or all of their profits to their stockholders. These payments are called dividends. The size of a dividend will vary with the short-term success of the company. Dividends are usually not paid during periods when a company is not profitable. While increases in value as seen daily can be volatile, dividends (when available) are much more consistent.

Stocks provide a high rate of return (on average, approximately 10 percent). However, the value of stock can change dramatically in a short period of time. For this reason, if you invest in stocks you should be investing for the long term.

Bonds

- Average rate of return: Approximately 6 percent
- Purpose: Set return
- Time span: Intermediate, typically four to ten years

Bonds are issued by the government, by corporations, and by financial institutions. When you buy a bond you are lending money to the issuer in exchange for a set amount of interest paid until a specific date, at which time the bond is said to mature and the principle is repaid. Typically, bonds pay interest every six months but other payment schedules are possible. Some bonds pay all of the interest on the date they mature.

Until a bond matures, its value will fluctuate because of market interest rates, which rise and fall based on the outlook for inflation. It may seem contradictory, but if interest rates go up, bond prices go down. If interest rates go down, bond prices go up. This occurs because a bond's interest rate is a set percentage of the value of the bond when it was issued. If during the life of the bond interest rates go down, the value of the bond goes up. This is because at this point in time it takes a bigger investment to get the same amount of interest. The opposite happens as interest rates go up, the bond becomes less valuable. Think of a teeter-totter, with bond values on one side and interest rates on the other.

However, if you buy an individual bond, the amount of your original investment is always returned to you on the bond's maturity date (unless the bond issuer defaults on the promise to pay you back). As a result, bond values are not as volatile as stocks. Because bonds give you a set rate of return for a known period, they can be especially valuable as a retirement investment. They are well suited for investing to obtain a predictable stream of income. But because bond returns on average are 5 to 6 percent, bonds should not be the major component of a long-term investment program.

Cash

- Average rate of return: Approximately 3 percent
- Purpose: Safe
- Time span: Short, typically three years or less

Some part of every portfolio is invested in cash. Cash investments are investments that are safe from loss of principal. Money market funds and certificates of deposit are both types of cash investments. These are the most stable investments, but they provide the least return on your money. Cash investments are a good place to hold your funds temporarily while you seek a better investment choice, or if you plan to take out the money in a relatively short period. Money in cash options is safe, but should not be left there for long. After two or three years, inflation will start to erode the purchasing power of your investment.

Plan-Provided Investments

Investing in most 401(k) plans does not require that you select your investments from the thousands of stocks and bonds listed in the business section of your newspaper. Instead your employer has made it simple for you by offering you a limited number of investment funds from which to choose.

Investment Funds

An investment fund is a pool of money invested to achieve a stated investment objective. By investing in a fund, rather than individual securities, you get professional management, diversification, and lower fees. Investing through a fund also gives you the flexibility and liquidity to switch easily from one investment to another. An investment fund is usually concentrated in a specific type of investment asset. For example, the cash investment in your plan will typically be a money market fund. A stock fund, also called an equity fund, invests primarily in stocks.

A 401(k) bond fund invests mostly in bonds. However, bond funds have a significant disadvantage for 401(k) investors. Unlike a bond, a bond fund never matures. This means that you may not get back the amount of your original investment, called your principal, if changes in interest rates reduce the value of bonds in your bond fund. On the other hand, if you invest in a bond fund when interest rates are falling you could earn a capital gain in addition to collecting the interest. Do not invest in a bond fund if you want an investment that will not decline in value.

Investment fund choices in your plan can be managed by a variety of sources, including professional investment managers, banks, insurance companies, broker-dealers, and mutual fund companies. Mutual funds are different because they are managed according to specific federal regulations by a company that registers its funds as mutual funds with the Securities and Exchange Commission.

In addition to stocks, bonds, and cash, you may also be able to invest in real estate. If you own your home, you are already a real estate investor. A real estate investment can increase in value and generate rental income. On the other hand, real estate investments are often hard to sell and require considerable management. The advantage of real estate is that it gives you another type of asset in which to invest in addition to stocks, bonds, and cash.

Real estate investing in a 401(k) is usually provided through an investment fund concentrating in real estate investment trusts (REITs). A REIT is a trust that purchases, owns, and manages real estate. REITs may also manage a portfolio of real estate loans.

Professionally Managed Accounts

If you do not want to direct how your 401(k) money will be invested, a professionally managed account may be the right option for you. Investment options that are professionally managed may also be called lifestyle, lifecycle, life stage, hybrid investment options or balanced funds, but do not be deceived by these misleading names. This is the simplest choice you can make because the professionally managed account will invest your 401(k) money for you. You will not have to spend your time in educational meetings, reading over your employer-sponsored choices, or calculating the best options.

A professionally managed account is not a single investment but a self-contained asset allocation plan that contains a diverse mix of investments. A professionally managed account is not another investment fund. Be cautious about investing some of your

401(k) money in investment funds and some in a professionally managed account. The investment strategies of the two approaches will overlap in unpredictable ways and could significantly reduce your overall investment return.

Be aware that some professionally managed programs will also customize an investment strategy for you that takes into account a variety of factors that include your age, risk tolerance, and retirement expectations. If this is the case, you may have to complete a questionnaire before your money will be invested.

Brokerage Windows

Some 401(k) plans let you invest in stocks, bonds, or mutual funds of your choosing as well as the funds that are part of your plan's menu. Using this option, you trade through a designated brokerage account (also called a window or open window account), just as you would use a broker outside the plan. Some companies will allow you to invest all of your plan assets this way, others will limit the amount of plan assets you can directly invest with a brokerage firm.

Here are some guidelines to follow when you want to use a brokerage firm to directly purchase the stocks of your choice.

- *Determine the fees you will be charged ahead of time.* Typically, a brokerage account carries an annual fee, but you will probably also pay transaction costs and commissions on each trade you make.
- *Remember to think long term.* Transaction costs and commissions mean the brokerage account takes a little bit of your retirement money with every transaction. Whether you are hitting the big time or hitting rock bottom, the brokerage account gets a cut.
- *Be cautious about purchasing a mutual fund through this account.* Mutual funds offered directly through your 401(k) may be far cheaper—either because your employer subsidizes part of the investments, or because a bundled arrangement with your

plan's service provider reduces or eliminates fees. When you purchase a mutual fund on your own, you get no discounts.

- *Know what stocks or kinds of stocks you want before you go to a broker.* You can do simple research on individual companies at the library and online. Remember that you are looking for a good long-term investment.

If your company is publicly traded, you will not be able to buy shares of your own company's stock from your 401(k) brokerage account. This is especially true if your 401(k) plan has company stock as an investment option or as a profit sharing contribution. Your company is required to make sure that no employees with special inside information about company activities take advantage of that information by investing in company stock.

Mutual fund windows

Some 401(k) plans let you invest in virtually any mutual fund you want, but not individual stocks or bonds. These are called mutual fund windows. Companies that offer only a mutual fund window do so to eliminate investments that might be available in the more flexible brokerage account that could result in a prohibited transaction or insider trading. The company might also use mutual fund windows instead of a brokerage window to ensure that investments in the plan are in a diversified fund.

7

Stable Value Funds

One of the advantages of participating in a 401(k) plan is the possible presence of a stable value investment option. Stable value is a fixed income investment, like a bond, but the value of your original investment amount does not change. For the fixed income aspect of your 401(k) asset allocation, stable value funds are an important investment choice because they provide a high rate of return with virtually no risk.

Like short-term or intermediate-term bond funds, stable value funds may be invested in U.S. government and agency securities, corporate bonds, and mortgage and asset-backed securities. Unlike bond funds, however, they may also be invested in interest-bearing contracts purchased directly from banks, insurance companies, or mutual funds, which guarantee to maintain the value of the principle and all accumulated interest. These also are called guaranteed investment contracts (GICs). The stability in all of these kinds of stable value funds is that they do not go down in value. By contrast, the value of bonds or bond funds can drop if interest rates increase, or rise if interest rates go down.

Stable Value Investments

Stable value fund investments are considered very steady and have remained at an average 6.1 percent rate of return for the past five years. Over the last 23 years, the highest average rate of return was 11.4 percent and the lowest was 5.9 percent, as shown in Figure 7.1. While stable value returns are subject to changes on a quarterly basis, they rarely fluctuate more than 1 percent a year. In fact,

FIGURE 7.1   Historical Rates of Return for Stable Value Funds

Year	Return	Year	Return
1978	8.5	1990	8.8
1979	8.4	1991	8.5
1980	9.4	1992	7.8
1981	10.1	1993	7.0
1982	11.4	1994	6.5
1983	11.2	1995	6.5
1984	12.0	1996	6.1
1985	11.9	1997	6.2
1986	10.9	1998	6.1
1987	9.8	1999	5.9
1988	9.0	2000	6.5
1989	9.1	2001	6.2

Stable Value annual returns from PSCA Annual Survey, 1980–1999. 2000 and 2001 numbers are from Hueler Companies.

stable value yields for the next year are fairly predictable and should be quoted to you by any fund you are considering as an investment.

Stable Value versus Other Funds

While the stable value option has been likened to bond funds and money market funds, stable value funds have the positive attributes of both kinds of investments with few drawbacks. Stable value investors receive interest income comparable to that earned on a short-term or intermediate-term corporate bond fund, but stable value provides more diversification. This allows for less market risk than bond funds, which have risen and fallen alongside equity investments. Stable value funds may also incur less expense than bond funds, which have an average expense ratio of 1 percent, compared to 0.3 percent for stable value funds. In comparison to money market funds, stable value investments have equal liquidity and stability, but significantly higher average interest rates (1 to 2 percent more).

While stable value investments provide a good rate of return, they are no substitute for stocks. However, when used in conjunction with equity investments, stable value funds lower the overall market volatility risk of your portfolio. Replacing the fixed income aspect of your asset allocation (such as bond funds) with stable value choices allows you to devote more of your assets to equity investments, which increases your return, without increasing your risk.

Transfers and Withdrawals

When you transfer your stable value assets into another fund in your 401(k), movement of your assets into a money market fund may be restricted, require transfer to an equity for a limited time first, or involve a penalty. These rules are used to prevent you from constantly switching in and out of stable value funds, as this defeats the purpose of the investment as a long-term generator of earnings.

In general, stable value investments have no withdrawal restrictions other than the plan withdrawal rules for 401(k). Stable value investors usually have access to their accounts at full value for withdrawals and transfers without penalty. However, because some stable value funds are purchased contracts, in special cases the plan itself may impose additional withdrawal restrictions to comply with the terms of the contract. This may delay a distribution of your funds when you leave the plan.

Who Invests in Stable Value?

Older plan participants invest a greater percentage of their 401(k) assets in the stable value option than younger employees. Why? For anyone nearing retirement, or retired but retaining their funds in their former employer's 401(k) plan, stable value funds make sense. These participants may not be able to keep as much of their investments in equity because of a shortened time horizon that makes them more vulnerable to short-term market fluctuations. At the same time, they need to earn a predictable rate of return that will provide them with income in retirement. At a time when participants are changing their asset allocation to more conservative choices, stable value funds provide security along with a steady, high rate of return. If you are approaching retirement, make sure to find out whether you can leave your 401(k) assets in your plan after you retire to take advantage of the stable value option. However, keep in mind that a 65-year-old retiree has a life expectancy of more than 20 years, and should not exclusively invest in a nongrowth investment.

Stable value funds are also useful for 401(k) participants who are uncomfortable with the ongoing ebbs and flows of the stock market. If a sudden downturn has made you feel insecure, having some of your money in a stable value fund may provide you with more confidence in the stability of your portfolio because the value of your original investment amount does not change.

If you are thinking of saving more in your 401(k) and are concerned about market volatility, put your new savings initially into the stable value fund. After you have been a 401(k) investor for a time, you will observe that stock market ups and downs are short term. Because of your stable value investment, you will feel more secure investing more of your 401(k) assets for long-term growth.

How Secure Are Stable Value Funds?

There are rules governing how companies can invest stable value funds, and there are contingencies so that 401(k) participants will be fully compensated. In isolated incidents where stable value fund assets were not immediately available, 401(k) participants were eventually made whole.

8

401(k) and Employee Ownership

If you work at a publicly traded company (one whose stock is listed on a stock exchange), or at one of the thousands of privately owned businesses that have given employees an ownership share in the company, read on.

Employee ownership occurs when you own your employer's stock through a company-sponsored program. This ownership aligns the interests of employees and employers for the benefit of both. For your employer, it generates workforce commitment, profitability, and growth. For you, it serves your long-term goals—savings, security, and wealth. Employee ownership is a way for you to share in your employer's financial success. Who better to own a piece of corporate America than you and the other employees at your company who collectively have the greatest impact on your company's bottom-line and long-term success.

Companies that share ownership with their employees do so through an employee stock ownership plan (ESOP), a 401(k) plan, or a plan that combines both (KSOP). The government encourages this practice by providing special tax advantages to both the company and the employee owner. Other employees enjoy ownership in company stock through programs such as stock purchase plans (section 423) or incentive stock option plans (section 421). Stock purchase and stock option plans are not considered tax-qualified retirement plans under federal law and are subject to separate tax code rules.

Employee Stock Ownership Plans (ESOPs)

An employee stock ownership plan (ESOP) is a qualified defined-contribution plan designed to provide employees with stock ownership in their company. ESOPs are required by law to invest primarily (at least 50 percent of its assets) in company stock. ESOPs can be either leveraged or nonleveraged. A leveraged ESOP has a special ability to borrow money to purchase the sponsoring corporation's stock. As the loan is repaid, the stock is allocated to the employee. This can be a useful financing technique for the company and its employees. It is most often used when an owner/manager of a company wishes to sell the company to his or her employees. A nonleveraged ESOP is like a deferred profit sharing plan in which the company contribution is made in the form of company stock or the company contribution is used to purchase company stock. It can also be allocated to the employees in the form of a 401(k) match.

ESOP Rules That Might Affect You

Because ESOPs receive special tax treatment, they are subject to a number of rules that do not necessarily apply to 401(k) and other defined-contribution plans.

- If an ESOP is offered at a privately held company, the company is required to annually obtain an outside appraisal of the value of the company stock. The appraisal is done by a person independent from the company who reports directly to the ESOP trustee.
- If you have participated in an ESOP for more than 10 years and are age 55 or older, you can diversify 25 percent of the value of your assets to prepare for your retirement. At age 60, with 15 years of participation, that figure increases to 50 percent. Some companies permit you to diversify at a younger age. When diversification is available to you, it can be accomplished by allowing you to transfer your cash account balance to your 401(k) plan, your IRA, or as a distribution to you.

- You may have the choice of using a dividend pass-through system, which means that you may be able to deposit the dividends pretax into your 401(k) plan or receive the dividend as taxable income.
- ESOPs must, by law, own the "best" company stock. The "best" company stock must have the greatest dividend and voting rights; for example, common stock or convertible preferred stock. The ESOP trustee is responsible for voting the shares held in the ESOP. However, there are special issues that may arise that require a direct vote by the participants of the ESOP. Publicly traded companies must allow participants to vote on issues that regular shareholders are allowed to vote on.

In many cases, owning company shares through an ESOP plan gives you a say in some of the choices your company makes. If you own company stock registered with the SEC, you may have the right to be a part of the governing process for some special company matters put to a vote of shareholders. If you own unregistered stock, your plan may have to solicit your approval or disapproval when your company is considering corporate matters that could affect your stock, including but not limited to:

- Merger or acquisition
- Recapitulation
- Reclassification
- Liquidation, dissolution or sale of substantial assets

Company Stock in a 401(k)

Many companies have chosen to provide employees with an ownership interest by offering company stock through their 401(k) plan. The company can accomplish this in two ways:

1. Your employer can combine an ESOP with a 401(k), creating a KSOP. In a KSOP, the company matches employee 401(k) contributions to the plan with a contribution of company

stock. As with a standard 401(k) plan, employee contributions are invested in various fund options offered by the plan. Some companies match employee contributions according to a fixed formula with contributions in company stock, but do not set up a formal ESOP to hold the company contributions. Other companies make their profit sharing matching contributions in company stock. In some cases, the company might place restrictions on how the stock vests or can be sold if it not publicly traded.

2. Your employer can permit you to purchase company stock with your plan assets, essentially making company stock one of the choices in your asset allocation plan.

If company stock is offered through your 401(k), your company must provide you with additional financial information. In the case of a publicly traded company, this usually takes the form of an annual report and, in some cases, quarterly updates. This financial disclosure is intended to empower you, as an investor, to make an informed investment decision about your overall retirement asset allocation model.

One caveat: Purchasing company stock through your 401(k) or receiving it from your employer's match is not like drawing from a bottomless well. Some companies limit the amount of company stock that you can own in your account. Once you have a percentage of your assets in company stock, for example 25 percent, you may not be allowed to accumulate additional shares.

The Benefits of Company Stock in a 401(k)

So how good is the company stock option in your 401(k)? The payoffs of ownership are potentially substantial, but involve risk. Indeed, when Microsoft Corporation went public and Cain Chemical, Inc. was acquired, the value of the company stock held in both firms' profit sharing plans soared—and catapulted to wealth hourly employees and executives alike. Ownership in your company's stock can provide this wealth to you in two ways:

1. When you receive profits distributed in the form of dividends
2. When your company has increased in value and your company stock value goes up

In essence, when the company is well run and profitable, you are included in that success.

Thanks to 401(k) plan regulations, investing 401(k) assets in company stock has additional benefits. Federal rules prohibit investment managers from taking a commission from the sale or purchase of company stock in a defined contribution plan, when the transaction is made directly with the company. Also, there are no investment management fees for 401(k) amounts invested in company stock. Reducing fees in these two ways significantly cuts costs, and can result in better long-term net returns for your 401(k) portfolio.

Another major benefit of owning company stock is the tax regulation known as the net unrealized appreciation exception (NUA), which provides a special tax advantage. This tax treatment provides that when you take a lump-sum distribution in company stock from your 401(k) plan, you initially pay regular income taxes on only the initial cost of the shares to the plan (called the *cost basis*) rather than on their current value. You do not pay tax on the value of the appreciation until you sell the stock, at which time you pay tax at the capital gains tax rate, even if you sell the stock one day after you receive it from the plan. This can be a substantial tax break if the current capital gains tax rate is considerably lower than the income tax rate you pay on other 401(k) distributions, which are taxed at ordinary income tax rates.

However, taking a lump-sum distribution in order to take advantage of NUA is not always the best approach. Keeping your accumulation tax-deferred may be more appropriate, depending on the situation. You should carefully evaluate this choice before making a decision. You may want to consult with a financial planner to determine what makes the most sense for you. If you decide that you want to take advantage of this tax benefit, your plan sponsor will need to record and track the cost basis of all stock contributed to your account. Most companies have excellent record-keeping support systems to help you when it is time to take a distribution from your 401(k) plan. Be advised that if you roll your company stock into an IRA, or you roll your stock distribution over into another 401(k) plan, you will not be able to take advantage of this special tax treatment.

Diversification

For many who have company stock in their 401(k) plan, the company stock is a substantial percentage of their total assets. In long-standing businesses, a substantial concentration in company stock can be a major bonus. You know that the company stock has been steady for many years, will most likely continue to rise, and you can deposit your dividends, if any are issued, into the plan on a tax-deferred basis.

However, if a company suffers hard times, the value of your stock will decrease. If you previously worked for an Internet start-up or dot-com company, you know that company stock may not always be a wise investment. Also, if your company should go out of business, you will lose all or most of the value in your company stock, which is what happened to employees of Enron that owned company stock. The bottom line is that an investment in company stock is focused and far less diversified than is a stock mutual fund, and such focus can lead to significant swings in value. Consider diversifying your retirement funds into several investments with different risk/reward characteristics.

If you want to diversify your portfolio so it has less company stock, you need to know the rules for your plan. If you are in an ESOP you may have investment restrictions. For example, you probably cannot diversify your company's contributions until you have reached age 55 and have worked for the company for 10 years. At age 60 with 15 years of participation in the ESOP, you have the right to diversify up to 50 percent of the value of your ESOP account balance.

In other plans, you may be able to exchange your company stock much earlier, sometimes even immediately. It is important to be aware of these rules so you can make the best long-term decisions for your own needs, taking into account the entire range of your retirement savings opportunities.

Chapter 10 of this book addresses the concept of asset allocation. Asset allocation is the process of dividing your retirement assets into different risk/reward types of investments. Company stock is a high-risk asset class. As you near retirement age, it is usually wise to diversify some of your retirement assets out of company stock into more conservative investment classes.

9

401(k) Investing
Easier Than You Think

401(k) investing is not as hard as you might think. Investing in your 401(k) means thinking long term and following a few simple rules. This chapter will give you the basic information you need to create a lifetime approach for investing and managing your money. Whether your retirement is 40 years away or on the horizon, why wait? Today is the day to take control.

Because we are all living longer, everything is changing—especially our work, how we spend our money, and how we save for the future. In addition, we face the challenge of the retirement of the baby boomer generation, which will put incredible strain on the retirement system. In 2029 when the youngest baby boomers reach age 65, it is likely that 100 million Americans will be 65 or older. At that time, 400,000 Americans will be at least 100 years old. As a result, we must all change the way we feel about money, and learn to think beyond our immediate needs. Living from paycheck to paycheck today is a good indication that you are not prepared for tomorrow. In fact, even putting money aside in savings is, by itself, not enough. To ensure that you are financially secure in retirement, you must become a lifetime investor.

Why should you become a lifetime investor? You cannot depend solely on others, including the government or your employer, to support you in retirement. The government's resources are limited. It can only provide an amount equal to what taxpayers can pay, divided by the number receiving benefits. At present, the number of those eligible to receive benefits from the government is growing rapidly. Employer support is limited as well. Companies must continually be profitable in a highly competitive economic world, which is an increasingly difficult challenge, and support for employees is dependent on current success.

The truth about money and retirement is that while your company and the government may help you, in the end, you alone are responsible for your financial success. This success requires a different approach to money, one that that makes long-term investing a cornerstone of your financial thinking. Long-term investing will help you win the race to retirement security because it is based upon two investment realities:

1. The mathematical certainty of compounding investment returns over time
2. The average long-term rate or return from investing in the stocks of America's publicly traded companies

The Power of Compounding

Ben Franklin said there are three comforts in old age: An old spouse, an old dog, and compound interest.

What is compounding? Simply put, it is continually keeping your investment return invested so it can earn additional returns. Why is it so powerful? Because as the return is earned, it is added to the original investment each year to form an ever-increasing base. This means that the return on your initial investment grows at a constantly rising rate. For example, Pat has $1,000 earning a compounded rate of 8 percent in his 401(k) plan. The first year, he will earn 8 percent ($80) on the original $1,000. In the second year he will earn 8 percent on the $1,000 and 8 percent on the $80 he earned as interest the year previous ($86.40). His account will be worth $2,158 after ten years, $4,660 after 20 years, and $10,062 after 30 years. If the 8 percent return on that same $1,000 is withdrawn and then deposited into a non-interest-bearing checking account, Pat will have $1,800 after ten years, $2,600 after 20 years, and $3,400 after 30 years. That's a difference of $6,662, a return of six times his original investment, just for investing long-term in a 401(k). This difference is illustrated in Figure 9.1.

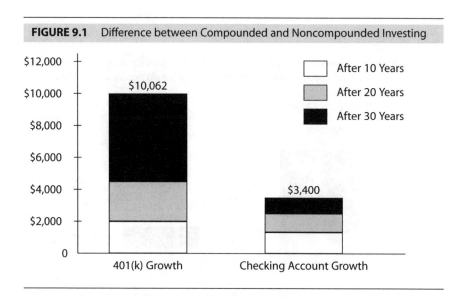

FIGURE 9.1   Difference between Compounded and Noncompounded Investing

Another result of compounding is that differences in rates of return are magnified. For example, Pat gets a compounded rate of return of 8 percent, while Gerry only gets a compounded rate of return of 4 percent. After 20 years, you would expect Pat to earn twice as much as Gerry. But in fact, Pat will earn three times as much, as shown in Figure 9.2. At 8 percent, Pat will earn $1,158 after ten years and $3,660 after 20 years. Gerry, with 4 percent rate of return, will earn $480 after ten years and just $1,191 after 20 years.

The predictability of compounding can also help you in your planning process. If you know your expected compounded rate of return, you can quickly estimate the number of years it will take to double an investment. To find the number of years, divide 72 by the rate of return. It is also easy to find the rate of return at which your investment must grow in order to double within a stated number of years. To do so, divide 72 by the number of years. Thus, if an investment is growing at a rate of 8 percent a year, it will double in nine years. At a 10 percent rate, it will double in 7.2 years. Similarly, if you want to double your money in four years, you must get an 18 percent compounded rate of return (72 ÷ 4 = 18).

Why does this work? The number of years it takes to double your money at a given interest rate is always approximately 72.

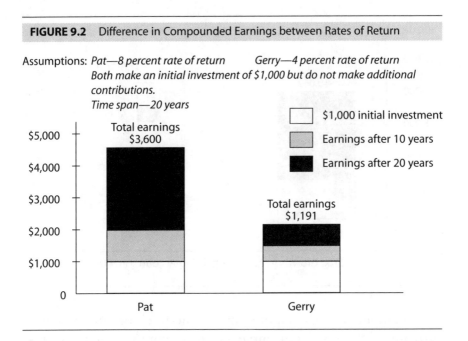

FIGURE 9.2   Difference in Compounded Earnings between Rates of Return

Assumptions: *Pat—8 percent rate of return*   *Gerry—4 percent rate of return*
Both make an initial investment of $1,000 but do not make additional contributions.
Time span—20 years

$1,000 initial investment

Earnings after 10 years

Earnings after 20 years

Total earnings
$3,600

Total earnings
$1,191

This is called the *Rule of 72*. Keep in mind that most investments do not grow at a steady rate, and that the Rule of 72 should only be used as a guide in setting long-term investment goals.

The Benefits of Investing in Stock

Letting your 401(k) investment return compound over time will help you build substantial retirement assets. But compounding alone is not enough. Your 401(k) investments must also earn an adequate rate to meet your needs. Historically, the most successful investment has been equity ownership of stock in America's publicly traded companies. Since 1926, such investments have earned a return of approximately 10 percent a year. Investments in stock have also outperformed bond investments by approximately 4 percent annually.

Properly investing in stocks for the long term is one of the safest investments you can make. Since 1926, stocks have never lost value in any 20-year period. Since 1959, they have not shown a loss in any 10-year period. Of course, if you are investing for short-term gain, stock investing can be risky.

Principles for Managing Your 401(k)

Your 401(k) will deliver retirement security to you if you take full advantage of both the power of compounding and the benefits of long-term stock investing. To do this, you must be guided by the following eight principles when you manage your 401(k):

1. Start with a plan.
2. Invest for the long term.
3. Diversify your investments.
4. Use reasonable assumptions.
5. Stay with your plan.
6. Rebalance at least annually.
7. Keep your money invested for as long as possible.
8. Understand the emotions of investing.

1. Start with a Plan

Each individual's personal and financial circumstances are unique. While common themes exist, we all have our own mix of economic goals, family responsibilities, personal expenses, earning power, and financial resources. Although retirement income may be available from many sources, the sources and amounts received from each vary by individual. Therefore, if you are to have the retirement experience you expect, you need to take control of your retirement future by developing and putting into practice a personal financial plan. Chapter 10 will help you do this.

2. Invest for Long-Term Gain

In a 401(k) plan, you invest for long-term gain because it will give you the greatest degree of predictability, it reduces investment risk, and it lets you take advantage of dollar-cost averaging.

Predictability. Investing for the long term lets you assume historical norms of return—for example, a long-term investment in equities results in a gain of approximately 10 percent per year. Investing for the long term also gives you more years to continuously build your return and take advantage of the mathematical certainty of compounding.

Reduces investment risk. You have two types of risk: the short-term risk of fluctuations in the value of your investments, and the long-term risk of inflation, which destroys purchasing power over time. Long-term investing limits the short-term volatility risk associated with equity ownership. In the short term, stocks go up and down, but over time stock market values tend to rise. Also, stock market values have grown approximately 6 percent more than the rate of inflation. This means that investing over the long term counters the affects of inflation risk.

Dollar cost averaging. When you invest long term you take advantage of an investment practice called dollar cost averaging. This practice allows you to use payroll deduction to save and invest a fixed amount in your account at regular intervals. When you use dollar cost averaging, your average cost per share over time is reduced because you buy more shares when the price drops, and fewer when it increases. The longer you use dollar cost averaging, the more effective it is.

3. Diversify Your Investments

When investing your 401(k) funds, you are not looking for just one place to put your money. On one hand, this means you are not trying to predict the next skyrocket stock to make yourself an overnight millionaire. On the other hand, you don't want to invest solely in one investment option because the market's ups and downs scare you. These two extremes, which seem quite different, actually cripple your investments in the same way. How? Because they unrealistically rely on one investment to do all the work. Your safe investment will never make enough to beat inflation, while your skyrocket stock could tank at any time. The best way to keep your money secure *and* make enough to provide for a successful retirement is to create a diversified investment portfolio. Diversifying your investments using an asset allocation strategy is explained in Chapter 10.

4. Use Reasonable Assumptions

Your goal is to become wealthy slowly. To meet this retirement goal, you need to have reasonable expectations. Specifically, this means you need to assume reasonable rates of return for your investments. Historically, stocks have returned approximately 10 percent a year and fixed return investments, like bonds, have returned 6 percent a year. If you maintain a properly diversified mix of investments, your 401(k) portfolio will include both stocks and fixed return investments. Over time, you should receive a rate of return that is the average of the returns of these two kinds of investments. When you estimate a rate of return for planning purposes, use 8 percent per year. If you assume a greater rate of return, you may fall short of your retirement goals because your savings rate was too low. Your assumptions help determine the amount you save, so by expecting reasonable rates of return (and saving more) the worst that can happen is early retirement.

5. Stay with Your Plan

The benefits of long-term investing can only be attained if you stick with a long-term plan. Without a long-term plan, you do not know where you are going, how you are going to get there, or even if you have arrived. Also, if you are constantly changing your mind about your asset allocation and your contribution rate, you don't really have a plan. Instead, you have become a short-term investor, subject to volatility risk and uncertainty.

6. Rebalance Periodically

Rebalancing is restoring your asset allocation to your original diversification plan. Short-term changes in the value of your stocks and fluctuating returns from fixed investments like bonds or stable value funds will result in a distribution of your assets that differs from what you have planned. If you originally put 60 percent of your money in stocks and 40 percent in bonds, that number can easily shift if one side of your investments does better than the other. Even more dramatically, if one side rises while the other falls, your allocation percentages can be far off the mark—for example, the allocation can change to 80 percent in stocks and 20 percent in bonds. If you do not periodically rebalance these assets, moving money around so that the percentage returns to your original allocation, you risk having the market make the change for you—when the market drops. These concepts are discussed in more detail in Chapter 10.

7. *Keep Your Money Invested for as Long as Possible*

Investing in a 401(k) will meet your retirement expectations only if you keep your 401(k) money invested until you retire. If you withdraw 401(k) money early, for example when you change jobs, you will lose both the principal and the future compounded return on the assets on which your retirement security will be based. This means you will have to save extraordinary amounts later in your career to make up the shortfall. Because you have lost the benefits of long-term compounding, you may not be able to save enough.

For example, if you take $5,000 out of your 401(k) when you change jobs rather than rolling the money over so it could continue to accumulate an 8 percent rate of return, your retirement fund could fall more than $50,000 short as a result of that one withdrawal.

8. *Understand the Emotions of Investing*

Ideally, your investment decisions will be based totally on the amount of time your money will stay invested. This means when you are young, your retirement investments should be aggressively invested for growth and you should ignore the fluctuations of the stock market. However, money and money-related decisions often affect people emotionally. Understand that fear and greed are normal emotions when it comes to investing. By acknowledging the danger they pose to your plan, you can be better prepared to avoid these pitfalls. While you may be making an intellectually correct decision about your money now, you need to consider whether you will be able to stay the course when the market changes against you or does much better than you expected in the short term. The amount of investment emotion you can stand is called your risk tolerance. You do not want to abandon your plan because you have an unexpected emotional response to short-term results. To prevent this from happening, take into account your own feelings about your financial matters when you plan your investment future. Consider using a professionally managed account if you have low risk tolerance, or if you tend to buy high and sell low.

401(k) Investment Concepts

As a 401(k) investor, there are basic concepts you should understand when you begin to invest. You've come across concepts like *asset allocation* and *rate of return* in your plan documents, investment magazines, and books. Many of these concepts were introduced in Chapter 9. Now it is time for you to join the ranks of those "in the know" about basic investing.

Asset Allocation

Your *assets* are comprised of all the money, investments, and property that you own. In investing, *asset classes* are investments that have similar characteristics (risk, capitalization, and predictability of return). Asset classes may be broadly defined (stocks, bonds, stable value, and cash) or more narrowly defined (large company or small company stocks).

Asset allocation is the process of dividing your assets among different types of investments. When you allocate your assets, you select the division of asset classes that is right for you and then invest your money accordingly. Typically, an asset allocation is stated in terms of percentages. For example, a 401(k) asset allocation plan might put 60 percent of your assets in stocks, 20 percent in stable value, 10 percent in bonds, and 10 percent in cash (money market fund). Your asset allocation should be determined by the investment strategy that you have identified to achieve your long-term financial goals.

Investment Return

Investment return is the increase (or loss) in value from each of your investments and on your investments as a whole. Investment returns are usually expressed as a rate (a percentage) and usually reported on an annual basis. Long-term rates of return are either the compounded rate of return over time on the investment, or the average percentage increase (or decrease) on the investment over a succession of one-year periods. Investment return rates allow you to compare the different performances of your investments and help trace your progress toward your long-term goal. Differences in long-term rates of return exist between different types of assets, as shown in Figure 10.1.

Annual rates of return reported for the investments in your 401(k) are normally net returns. This means that the fees for managing your investments are subtracted from your gains or added to your losses prior to the calculation of the annual return. The rates of return for the investments in 401(k) plans are usually stated for the most current one-year, three-year, five-year, and ten-year periods. Remember that as a 401(k) investor, you are looking for an average rate of return from all your investments combined over the long term, and that long-term return statistics are more reliable than last year's performance.

Risk

There are many types of risk. The risk that your investment will fall in value in the short term is *volatility risk*. The risk that your

---

FIGURE 10.1   Approximate Long-Term Rates of Return for Different Types of Investments

Type of Investment	Approximate Long-Term Rate of Return
Stocks (in general)	10 percent
Stable Value Fund	6 percent
Long-Term Bonds	6 percent
Treasury Bills	3 percent
Money Market Fund	3 percent

---

investment will lose its purchasing power because of inflation over the long term is *inflation risk*. The risk that the investment will become worthless is *investment risk*. Investment risk is a consideration when you are investing in stocks and corporate bonds. The most aggressive investments are said to carry the most volatility risk (and the most potential gain), as they are likely to rise and fall quickly in value. They also carry the most investment risk.

There are other types of risk as well. For example, *currency risk* is the risk that the exchange rate between the American dollar and the money of other countries will change in a way that will reduce the value of investments in non-American companies or for non-American bonds. Finally, there is *emotional risk*. This is the risk that an investor, after making a long-term asset allocation decision, will not be able to stay with that decision when short-term results are disappointing. In fact, the risk is that the investor will react emotionally and act unwisely.

Risk management is an important component of any investment program. There are two major factors in determining how risk should be managed. The first is your *investment time horizon*. The longer your time horizon, the more time you have to wait out the short-term ups and downs of the stock market. This means you need have little concern about volatility risk but much concern about the eroding effect of inflation. For example, when you are younger you can invest more in stocks which are volatile but whose long-term return will protect your investments from inflation risk. If you are close to retirement and will soon begin taking withdrawals from your retirement savings, you need to reduce your volatility risk by directing a greater amount into fixed income investments.

The second factor you need to consider as you plan to manage risk is your *short-term comfort level*. Investors are said to be aggressive, moderate, or conservative depending on their risk tolerance (the amount of short-term risk they can bear emotionally). If you believe that you will have an urgent need to sell if you see the value of your investments fall, you should be more conservative in your choices. On the other hand, you may be able to strengthen your ability to stay the course when short-term circumstances go against you. You can do this by learning more about investing either on your own or by talking to professionals. Either way, the better your understanding of how investing works, the more comfortable you will be with your long-term investment decisions.

As an investor it is important to understand the *risk-versus-reward ratio*. Basically, the greater your investment concentration in one or a few stocks, the greater your opportunity for gain, but the greater the chance that you will experience a substantial loss. If all of your money is invested in the stock of one company, you have the opportunity for great gain as some companies increase enormously in value. On the other hand, if the company in which you invest goes out of business, you will lose all of your investment. Investing in at least 50 stocks makes it less likely that you will have a big loss, but also less likely that you will have a big gain. Because you can plan on the long-term power of compounding, you do not need to take the extraordinary risks necessary to get big gains when you invest. You can afford to reduce your investment risk by diversifying your investments.

Diversification

To give yourself the greatest protection from risk you should diversify among asset classes (stocks, bonds, stable value, and cash). This is because, historically, when some asset classes have done well others have done poorly. If you have investments in all asset classes you reduce your risk without greatly reducing your long-term rate of return. The chart in Figure 10.2 shows comparative returns for different asset classes.

It is also important to diversify within an asset class. This divides your money devoted to that asset class between a number of funds that respond to the market differently. Large company stocks may move in a different direction than small company stocks, and stocks with dividends can withstand a stormy market better than those without. Each of your investments should also have a different rate of return and risk. Thus, diversity ensures investment success over the long run with the lowest amount of risk.

Diversification can also enhance your investment return. It does so by permitting you to invest a greater amount in a more risky and better-returning investment. Let's say you have two investment

FIGURE 10.2	Investment Returns

BOND: Lehman Brothers Aggregate Bond Index includes U.S. government, corporate, and mortgage-backed securities with up to 30-year maturities.
INT'L: The Morgan Stanley Capital International Index measures the performance of Europe, Australia, and Far East stock markets.
SC: The Russell 2000 Index measures U.S. small capitalization stock performance.
S&P: The S & P 500 Index measures U.S. large capitalization stock performance.
SV: Stable value annual returns from PSCA Annual Survey respondents, 1980–1999. 2000 and 2001 numbers are from Hueler Companies.

Year	Highest Percentage							Lowest Percentage	
1980	SC	38.6	S&P	32.5	INT'L	22.6	SV	9.4	BOND	2.7
1981	SV	10.1	BOND	6.3	SC	2.0	INT'L	−2.3	S&P	−4.9
1982	BOND	32.7	SCE	25.0	S&P	21.6	SV	11.4	INT'L	−1.9
1983	SC	29.1	BOND	23.7	S&P	22.6	SV	11.2	INT'L	8.9
1984	BOND	15.2	SV	12.0	INT'L	7.4	S&P	6.3	SC	−7.1
1985	INT'L	56.1	S&P	31.7	SCE	31.0	BOND	22.13	SV	11.9
1986	INT'L	69.5	S&P	18.7	BOND	15.0	SV	10.9	SC	5.7
1987	INT'L	24.6	SV	9.8	S&P	5.3	BOND	2.8	SC	−8.8
1988	INT'L	28.3	SC	24.9	S&P	16.6	SV	9.0	BOND	7.9
1989	S&P	31.7	SC	16.3	BOND	14.5	SV	9.1	INT'L	10.5
1990	BOND	9.0	SV	8.8	S&P	−3.1	SC	−19.5	INT'L	−23.5
1991	SC	46.1	S&P	30.5	BOND	16.0	INT'L	12.1	SV	8.5
1992	SC	18.4	SV	7.8	S&P	7.6	BOND	7.4	INT'L	−12.8
1993	INT'L	35.6	SC	18.9	S&P	10.1	BOND	9.8	SV	7.0
1994	INT'L	7.8	SV	6.5	S&P	1.3	SC	−1.8	BOND	−2.9
1995	S&P	37.9	SC	28.4	BOND	18.5	INT'L	11.2	SV	6.5
1996	S&P	23.0	SC	16.5	SV	6.1	INT'L	6.0	BOND	3.6
1997	S&P	33.4	SCE	22.4	BOND	9.6	SV	6.2	INT'L	1.8
1998	S&P	28.6	INT'L	20.0	BOND	8.7	SV	6.1	SC	−2.6
1999	INT'L	27.0	SC	21.3	S&P	21.0	SV	5.9	BOND	−0.8
2000	BOND	11.6	SV	6.5	SC	−3.0	S&P	−9.1	INT'L	−14.0
2001	SV	6.0	BOND	4.6	SC	1.0	S&P	−13.0	INT'L	−22.6

	Highest Average Annual Percentage			Lowest Average Annual Percentage	
BOND	4 times	2 times	6 times	4 times	5 times
INT'L	7 times	2 times	2 times	4 times	8 times
SC	4 times	8 times	4 times	2 times	4 times
S&P	5 times	4 times	9 times	3 times	1 time
SV	2 times	6 times	1 time	9 times	4 times

choices in your 401(k) plan: Choice A, which invests half in a fixed investment returning 6 percent annually and half in stock which returns 10 percent annually; and Choice B, which invests in only one investment returning 8 percent. If you invest $40,000, how will each investment choice fare after 20 years?

Choice A $20,000 @ 6% for 20 years = $64,142
            $20,000 @ 10% for 20 years = $134,549
                                    TOTAL $198,691
Choice B $40,000 @ 8% for 20 years   TOTAL $186,438

Rebalancing

If you do not periodically rebalance the assets in your 401(k) back to their original allocation percentages, you risk having the markets make the allocation for you. This is because without periodic rebalancing the better performing asset classes will become a greater and greater portion of your overall portfolio over time.

Early 401(k) critics stated that employees would overtrade their accounts and attempt to time the market. They predicted disastrous consequences both for individual employees and the retirement system. To paraphrase one of my good friends from Alabama, "That dog just didn't hunt." In fact, most 401(k) plan participants have done just the opposite. They do not activity manage their accounts enough.

Seventy-five percent of employees who join a plan choose four or fewer fund options in which to invest their contributions—which they seldom change. The allocation of options is shown in Figure 10.3.

FIGURE 10.3 Number of Investment Options Held by Participants (2000)

Number of Investment Options	Percent of Participants
One	25 percent
Two	18 percent
Three	18 percent
Four	14 percent
Five or more	25 percent

From *Building Futures Volume III: How Workplace Savings Are Shaping the Future of Retirement—A Report on Defined Contribution Plans,* Fidelity Investments, 2001.

Even older employees, those with the largest account balances, typically do not make changes in how their balances are allocated. As you can see in Figure 10.4, in 2000 most participants made no adjustments to their accounts.

Further, most participants do not respond to market volatility. For example, on August 31, 1998, only 0.46 percent of participants changed their balance allocations. This was the day when the Dow dropped 513 points, its biggest one-day point loss of the year, and 1 billion shares were traded for the first time on the New York Stock Exchange. There seems to be no relationship between increases and decreases in the Dow and participation reallocation of 401(k) account balances.

It is good that throughout the stock market volatility of the past several years, plan participants have, for the most part, stayed the course, not reallocating their 401(k) assets, instead embracing an in-it-for-the-long-haul ideology and avoiding attempts to market time. However, being too passive also has negative consequences. The problem is not that participants have traded too much in their accounts, it's that they have neglected to rebalance and have, therefore, traded too little.

There are two ways to rebalance your portfolio: (1) reallocating your existing account balance back to your original allocation percentages, or (2) changing how your future contributions are invested. The more precise way is the first, the reallocation of your existing account balance.

Basically, the more time you have until you need to access your retirement money, the more important it is that you rebalance your account. Let's assume that based on your calculations you should have $10,000 allocated to a large cap growth fund. When you check

---

FIGURE 10.4   Percent of Participants Who Made Investment Changes in 2000

Number of Investment Options	Percent of Participants
None	74 percent
One	15 percent
Two	5 percent
Three	2 percent
Four or more	4 percent

your account balance, you find that the market increased so much the prior year that you now have $15,000 in the large cap fund. You then need to switch (i.e., rebalance) $5,000 from the large cap growth fund and move it into any of your other funds where there is less money than targeted. The purpose is to start every year with the same percentages of your assets in each investment as provided in your investment strategy.

Some other tips for rebalancing:

- *Your stock/bond/stable value/cash division is key.* While changes within each type of investment (such as between your large company stocks and small company stocks) should also be rebalanced, maintaining the division among your asset classes should be your first priority. If you grow too heavily into stocks you risk the impact of a market drop.
- *Never let investments change by more than 25 percent.* While we encourage making annual rebalancing a healthy habit, it is more important to keep an ongoing eye on your allocation and change it whenever the increase (or decrease) is too great.
- *Sell winners, buy losers.* When one investment does extremely well and you must rebalance, use your gain to bring up the slack in the slower investment. This keeps you from being too heavily invested in the winning fund, which could drop suddenly. That slower investment won't earn you a big return, but it will lock in your gains and keep your money secure.
- *Diversify.* If you do not have a good mix of different investments to start, rebalancing cannot help you reach your retirement goals. Keep in mind that diversification, dollar cost averaging, and rebalancing take advantage of short-term volatility to help make you a more successful investor.

As an investor, you make money by buying when prices are low and selling when prices are high. In addition to helping you stay in control of you portfolio, periodic rebalancing of your 401(k) assets has the benefit of forcing you to sell high and buy low. That's because at the point when rebalancing occurs, the best performing asset is sold and the worst performing asset is bought. Because of this, annual rebalancing can increase your 401(k) return over time.

Fees

While your employer may pay some fees associated with the administration of your 401(k), others could be charged to your 401(k) account. Fees for the investment management of your plan assets are typically the largest 401(k) plan fees that you will pay. Typically, these fees are an annual percentage of the amount of assets managed and are stated in terms of basis points. Each basis point is 1/100 of 1 percent. In other words, 100 basis points is a 1 percent fee. The level of the investment management fees for the options offered in your plan will likely vary, depending on the type of investment management and the nature of the investment fund managed.

You should always consider fees when you decide which options of your plan in which to invest. Fees that are charged against your account lower your plan investment return. This reduces the total amount of assets you will accumulate for retirement. For example, both Gerry and Pat get the same rate of return (8 percent) on their plan investments. However, Gerry pays 100 basis points in fees but Pat pays only 50 basis points in fees. After 20 years, Pat will have a total of $424,785, or $37,817 more than Gerry, as shown in Figure 10.5.

If your plan permits you to direct the investment of assets in your account, your plan administrator will provide you with information describing the investment management fees and other fees associated with each of the investment options available to you. In many cases, this information will be called a *prospectus*. This information may also be available on your company's Web site.

FIGURE 10.5   Difference in Asset Growth Due to Fees

	Gerry	Pat
Plan assets	$100,000	$100,000
Annual return	8 percent	8 percent
Fees	100 basis points	50 basis points
Period	20 years	20 years
Total Assets	$386,968	$424,785
Difference		$37,817

Most fund options in 401(k) plans do not charge fees in addition to the annual investment management fee. However, if you work at a small company, the fund options in your plan may have sales charges that are paid when you invest. These are known as *front-end loads* or *commissions*. Some funds may charge when you sell. These charges may be called *back-end loads*, *deferred sales charges* or *redemption fees*. A front-end load is deducted up front and, therefore, reduces the amount of your initial investment. A back-end load is determined by how long you keep your investment. There are various types of back-end loads, including some which decrease and eventually disappear over time.

Some funds are *actively managed*. This means they have an investment advisor who researches, monitors, and actively trades the holdings of the fund in order to obtain a higher than average rate of return. Actively managed funds generally have higher investment management fees because they provide continuous management support and because active management requires more trading, which generates more brokerage charges.

Some funds are *passively managed*. Passively managed funds seek to obtain the investment results of an established market index, such as the Standard and Poor's 500, by duplicating the holdings included in the index. Passively managed funds require little research or trading activity. As a result, passively managed funds usually have lower management fees.

Your employer is required to ensure that fees paid to plan investment managers are reasonable in light of the level and quality of services they provide. If you have questions regarding the rates of return or fees for your plan's investment options, ask your plan administrator for an explanation.

Finally, fees should be only one of the factors you consider when choosing among your plan's investment options. Compare the net returns of your investment choices and their risks. Higher investment management fees do not necessarily mean better performance, nor are options with lower fees necessarily better.

Your Financial Plan

To take control of your retirement future, you need to develop and execute a long-term financial retirement plan. Consider how you planned your most recent driving vacation. First you choose a destination. Next you mapped a route. Then, following your map, you drove to your vacation spot. Without such a process you will not know how much to save or how to manage your investments. Even more important, having a plan helps you stay focused on the long term, even when you are in unfamiliar territory. Like the ball in a pinball machine, without a personal financial retirement plan you will bounce from event to event until short-term needs and wants overwhelm any long-term investing discipline.

Taking control of your retirement future with your 401(k) plan has four parts:

1. Defining your goal
2. Developing your plan
3. Implementing your plan
4. Monitoring your progress

Defining Your Goal

To begin the retirement planning process, you need to determine your retirement savings target and put it in writing. Writing down a specific financial objective not only ensures the clarity of your goal, it also helps motivate you to stick with that goal.

The first step in determining your savings target requires that you realistically estimate your expenses in retirement and project your expected life span. This approach recognizes that your financial needs, goals, expectations, and the time you will live in retirement are special to you. The best financial plan you can make will be based upon your unique circumstances. This means you need to do a little homework.

Plan for Life Events

Start by identifying any purpose for which you will need money in retirement. Obviously, you will want a stream of income to pay your normal living expenses. This means thinking about your standard of living, which will include your income bracket and the amount of money you spend on enjoying life. The little extras—such as a meal out at a favorite restaurant, a massage, or visits to your family—break up your routine, serve as a reward for all your hard work, and, in essence, make life worth living. Do you want to continue to experience these treats in retirement? Of course! In fact, before you consider groceries, the cost of gas, or house payments, you are probably imagining your retirement funds paying for the fun activities. If that is the case, you need to judge how much retirement money you will need to be able to afford the important basics and still have money in reserve.

You also need to list the major expenditures you expect to make after you retire. Will you be traveling around the world and presenting your grandchildren with lavish gifts? Are you going to buy a retirement home, continue your education, help older parents, or pay off your current mortgage? Be sure to include in your list the most common financial problem in retirement: the expense of health care, which can overwhelm your savings if unexpected.

If you consider your current state of health, your personal health care regime (or lack of it), and the health your parents experienced in their elder years, you can extrapolate out an image of your health in retirement and whether you will eventually need long-term health care. It is far better to be honest with yourself and plan ahead, than to find yourself financially short at a time when you most need it.

Social Security

There may be uncertainty about how much Social Security will provide you, but you should receive something. To determine how much you have accrued in your account under current rules, call the Social Security Administration at 800-772-1213 to request a copy of your Personal Earnings and Benefit Estimate Statement.

You should also consider the age when you become eligible to receive Social Security benefits as you make your financial retirement plan. Under current rules your eligibility depends on the year in which you were born. See Figure 11.1 to determine your age of eligibility.

You can begin collecting benefits early, at age 62, but your benefit will be reduced by up to 30 percent (the later the year you were born, the greater the reduction). If you do want to work after retirement, you may be better off waiting until age 70 to collect Social Security. To encourage you to delay taking Social Security past your eligibility date, you are also offered an incentive for every year you wait until you are 70. This bonus, called the Delayed Retirement Credit, increases your Social Security benefit 5.5 to 8 percent (depending on the year you were born).

FIGURE 11.1   When Are You Eligible to Receive Social Security?

Year of Birth	Age of Eligibility
Before 1938	65
1938	65 and 2 months
1939	65 and 4 months
1940	65 and 6 months
1941	65 and 8 months
1942	65 and 10 months
1943–1954	66
1955	66 and 2 months
1956	66 and 4 months
1957	66 and 6 months
1958	66 and 8 months
1959	66 and 10 months
1960 and later	67

Your Life Expectancy

Setting your retirement savings target requires that you predict your life expectancy. This is not as hard as it seems. You can make a pretty good estimate by reviewing your family history and by considering the average life span of Americans in general. While the U.S. government estimates that the average life span is now 76 years, this includes the 21 percent of the population who die before age 65. Using current estimates, you will likely live to be older than 76. Men who live to see age 65, usually live to 84, while women reaching 65, usually live to 88. The average life span is also lengthening every year, so add a year or two to your estimate just to be safe.

A Family Plan

If you are married, your retirement savings will have to provide for both of you, so you and your spouse should develop a retirement plan together. In addition, both spouses may be able to contribute financially to achieve your family's retirement savings goal. If you are married, you should coordinate your 401(k) participation as discussed in Chapter 4.

Tools to Help You

There are resources to help you plan, make the right decisions, and track your investments. Following are sources you might look to for assistance.

Modeling tools and software. In retirement, some of your expenses will go up, while others will go down. To determine a retirement savings goal that is more precise than a guess, you can use a modeling program. You may also look in the materials given to you by your plan's investment provider for what is usually called a retirement planning calculator. Worksheets or interactive programs are available on your employer's Web site and nearly all Web sites that provide financial information.

Personal advice and education. Your company may provide some form of assistance when you are making decisions about your plan. This could come in the form of educational materials, seminars for you and your coworkers, or Web-based information, which will help you make more informed decisions. Your plan may also provide access to a financial planner who will work with you one on one, looking at your particular situation to provide advice just for you. Always find out if you will be paying a fee for such assistance (it can come directly out of your plan assets). If you would like to seek out your own financial guidance, see Chapter 16 for more information on picking a financial planner.

Set a Savings Goal

Now that you've considered both your retirement expenses and how long you will live in retirement, you can set your savings goal. You need a specific goal, which you should set as a percentage of your final pay. To determine this percentage, take the following four steps:

1. *Find your final salary.* Estimate what your salary will be at the time of your retirement by adjusting your current income for expected salary increases from now until you retire.
2. *Divide your expenses by your final salary.* Take the amount you expect to spend annually on everyday expenses and divide it by your expected final salary. This will identify the percentage of your final income that you will need in retirement and provide the basis of your savings target. You can use this percentage of final pay with modeling software or financial calculators to determine the savings and investment approach that will give you the retirement assets necessary to generate this level of income for you. As an alternative, a simpler way to project your expenses in retirement is to simply take 70 percent of your current salary.
3. *Divide your extras by your final salary.* Take the amount you expect to spend annually on extraordinary items during retirement, like that around-the-world cruise, and divide that

number by your final salary amount. This identifies the percentage of final income you will need for items that are extra.

4. *Add your percentages.* Add your extras percentage to your everyday percentage and you will know how much of your final salary you need to save.

A simpler target—ten times final pay. Does the above approach seem complicated and difficult? Perhaps expressing your retirement goal as a percentage of final salary, which is the basis of so many calculators, seems confusing and irrelevant. There is an alternative: ten times final pay. This approach expresses your goal in lump sum terms, like other aspects of your financial life, such as checking accounts, mortgage owed, and even taxes.

Again, start by determining what your salary will be at the time of your retirement. Then, multiply that amount by a specific number, for example ten, to set your retirement goal. For example, if you anticipate earning $50,000 in the last year before you retire you would set a retirement savings target of $500,000.

Why ten times final pay? Approximately seven times your projected final salary will likely pay for a lifetime annuity. This annuity, when combined with Social Security, will give you an annual income of 100 percent or more of your final pay after you retire. If you save ten times final pay, the extra three times your final salary can remain invested to provide protection against inflation for your annuity. This extra amount can also provide a financial reserve for emergencies and any extra unplanned expenditures that you may have.

Remember that the retirement savings goal that you set may change as you get closer to retirement. However, you need a specific goal when you begin saving, and at every step of the way, if you are to maintain the long-term financial discipline necessary to be financially secure when you retire.

Developing Your Plan

Now that you have determined the retirement goal you are trying to achieve, you are ready to develop an action plan to meet that goal.

Determine Your Current Financial Status

Do you know how much debt you have, how much income you make, or where all that money is actually going? If you do not know where you stand now, you will not be able to estimate where you'll be in the future. You may be a two-income family spending money on your kids, your mortgage, and your return to school to brush up on your skills. Perhaps you are single with car payments, rent, school loans, and credit card debt. No matter how much you are earning or where you are in life, you have unique money management habits, beliefs, and skills that affect you. The key is to realistically view how you handle the flow of your assets. Once you do so, you can continue the good habits that will bring you success and change any habits that block the road ahead.

Identify Your Sources of Retirement Income

Just as you have considered all the ways you will spend money and how much you currently have, you should also have an accurate list of all the ways you will build long-term wealth. Sources of retirement income may include:

- Personal savings
- Equity in your home
- 401(k) assets
- Other employer-provided retirement plans, including traditional pension plans
- Government programs such as Social Security
- Continued employment
- Inheritances

Pick an Investment Mix That Fits

There are many options in investing, and you must pick the mix that's right for you. This should be composed of a diversified mix of stocks or stock funds and what are called *fixed investments* (i.e., bonds, stable value, and cash). That mix will be dependent on how long your money can stay invested and your emotional tolerance for short-term market volatility. It should also be based upon reasonable expected returns. A diversified mix for most people should provide a long-term compounded rate of return of 8 percent. There are modeling tools and professional assistance that will help you make the determination that is right for you. If you want to use an expected rate of return in one of these modeling programs before you pick your mix, I suggest you use 8 percent.

Think Long Term

Your investment plan should focus on the long term. A long-term approach to investing your 401(k) plan assets will give you the best rate of return. It will also give you predictability, reduce your exposure to short-term volatility, protect you from the eroding effects of inflation, and give you the benefits of dollar cost averaging.

Short-term declines in the stock market may make you feel uncertain. The market has cyclical peaks and dips, so over the many years that you invest, the market (much like the ocean) will ebb in and out. But a long-term time horizon can withstand both ups and downs with a steady rate of growth over time. Saving consistently for retirement and investing long term will put you on the right track for a financially secure retirement.

Contribute Enough

The final stage in creating your plan is determining how much you need to contribute. Remember, it is not enough to simply make a plan for retirement. You must also contribute the right amount while you are working in order to make that plan work. When deciding how much to contribute, remember the following principles:

- *Save enough now to avoid having to save more later.* The earlier you start saving the less you will have to save in the future. If you are 22 and delay saving one year, you may have reduced your future retirement balance by $100,000. This means you will have to save more later to make up the shortfall.

- *Save consistently.* Saving consistently keeps you in line with your long-term plan and lets you take advantage of dollar cost averaging.
- *Make the most of your company's contribution.* Your employer contribution is more retirement savings for you, all of it a free benefit for simply making your own contributions.

Let's say you have decided to contribute 3 percent of pay. First, determine the long-term rate of return you will most likely receive from your investment strategy. Then calculate how much you will have at retirement, given your rate of return and your contribution rate (you can use a financial calculator to help you). Will it meet your retirement goal? Are you maximizing your employer match? If not, you can adjust your contribution amount before you even begin to save.

What if you need to increase your contribution, but don't feel like you can afford to? The end result of your plan—the ultimate dollar goal—may call for modest changes in your current behavior. Decreasing expenses or choosing to work for an employer that allocates a larger share of the compensation dollar to your 401(k) plan are among the factors you may have to consider. Unless you save enough, you may have to reduce your standard of living in retirement and even continue working in your golden years just to stay afloat. Wouldn't you rather cut back on a few luxuries now (like that expensive cappuccino every morning) rather than cutting back on some basics (like food and clothing) later?

Another approach is to start at a level you feel comfortable with and slowly increase your contribution rate each year. For example, suppose you need to save 10 percent of pay. If your company matches 6 percent of pay, start your contribution rate at that level. This is free money, take advantage of it immediately. For each of the following years, raise your contribution rate by 1 percent. This strategy allows you to achieve your goal through gradual change.

Implementing Your Plan

Once you have determined where you want to go and how to get there, your 401(k) makes it easy. Just tell your employer how much you want to save and how you want your savings invested. Your company will do the rest. However, once you have invested your funds, you cannot just sit back, relax, and let your investments grow all by themselves. Managing your plan will require you to keep your long-term goals in sight.

You will need to rebalance your investments back to your original investment strategy at least annually. Every year you should begin with the same percentage of your assets in each of your investments as provided in your investment plan. By rebalancing once a year, you can easily and painlessly adapt your retirement course to the ever-changing winds of investing in order to secure your retirement future. It's as simple as that!

Also, over the years you may have to monitor and adjust your spending, saving, and investment strategies to take advantage of or to defend against changing personal financial situations. A good rule of thumb is to reevaluate your retirement savings plan once a year to adjust to any changes right away, rather than trying to close the gap when you are close to retirement.

Someone who considers day-to-day or month-to-month survival as "success" does not save or plan for the long term. But when you implement a long-term retirement savings plan in a 401(k) and your assets begin to build, you will understand that you too can have wealth and share in the profits of the American corporate system. In fact, the growth of your assets may challenge your personal beliefs about money by opening you to new possibilities and enabling you to look to the future.

Monitoring Your Progress

The only certain thing about the future is change. This means that you need to periodically monitor your progress to make sure you are on track. Have your life circumstances or goals changed? Do you need to develop a new plan or modify your old one? Like rebalancing, you must do this on a regular basis. It would be wise to evaluate your progress at least every five years.

12

When You
Change Jobs

You may change jobs several times during your career. In fact, it is now common for an employee to work for seven employers before retirement. But what happens to your 401(k) plan assets when you change jobs? Must you take the money out of the plan and pay taxes? Do you have to start at zero with each new employer? The answer is a resounding no! The key to building a financially successful retirement is keeping your 401(k) assets in a tax-sheltered plan during your entire working career. For that reason, the government provides you with three tax-free options when you leave your job:

1. Move your assets over into your new employer's tax-sheltered plan.
2. Leave your assets in your old employer's plan.
3. Move your assets directly into an individual retirement account (IRA).

This flexibility of options, which allows you to keep your assets in your old plan or move them to a new tax-sheltered plan according to your own individual needs, is called portability. When your move your assets into another tax-sheltered plan, be it an employer-offered plan or an IRA, it is called a rollover. In each of these cases, both your contributions and your earnings keep their special status, so you do not have to pay taxes.

Most plans give you 30 days to decide what to do with your plan assets when you leave an employer. Your plan administrator must send you a notice of this time deadline, which will inform you of your choices and provide you with the proper paper or

Web-based forms. Once you receive notice, the clock starts ticking. If you make no choice after 30 days, you may be forced to take your funds as a distribution if your balance is less than $5,000. This means facing a 20 percent income tax withholding and regular income tax if you do not roll over your distribution within 60 days from the date you receive the funds. If you are younger than age $59\frac{1}{2}$ on April 15 of the year you take the distribution, it also means a 10 percent early withdrawal federal income tax penalty. Be sure to make your decision and fill out your forms before this deadline expires.

Your new employer's plan is usually the best option, because it provides you with the most control and consolidates your new contributions with your old assets into one easily accessible account. In addition, 401(k) plans provide prescreened, high-quality investments and the possibility of a loan in a time of need, while an IRA does not. But if you do not have the option of a rollover into a new employer's plan, your former employer's plan is an excellent runner-up.

Your New Employer's Plan

When you change employment, your 401(k) assets may be eligible for rollover into your new employer's plan. However, a 401(k) plan is not right for all companies and may not be offered at your new job. Certain nonprofit organizations provide 401(k)-like plans, such as a 403(b) or 457 plan, to help their workers save for retirement. Other companies may offer plans very different from a 401(k), for example, a defined benefit plan or a 403(a) annuity, for their employees. Fortunately, your 401(k) assets may be rolled over into one of a number of different employer plans, including:

- 401(k) plans
- 403(b) plans
- 457 plans
- Profit sharing plans
- Money purchase plans
- Defined benefit plans

- 403(a) annuity plans
- Stock bonus plans

However, if your new employer provides one of these plans, it is still not legally required to accept your rollover money. While almost all plans do accept 401(k) rollovers, some may not accept money that was contributed after-tax or they only may accept rollovers at certain times. Before you make any decision about what to do with your money, be sure to find out if rollovers are accepted and if any restrictions exist. Also ask your new plan administrator for the necessary forms to process the rollover into your new 401(k).

Your Previous Employer's Plan

Sometimes leaving your money in your former employer's plan is the right option. Your new employer may require that you work for six months or a year before being eligible for your new plan. Or you may still be in the process of job searching and not yet have a new plan. In either case, if you leave your assets in your former employer's plan you can then move the money directly into a new 401(k) when you are ready. In addition, if your employment ends due to a temporary layoff, your employer may rehire you after a short break. Keeping your assets in your employer's plan will allow you to continue participation without hassle.

If you would like to keep your money in your former employer's plan, be aware of the following considerations:

- *Minimum amount.* If you have less than $5,000 in your account, you may not be able to keep your assets in the plan. According to the law in effect in 2001, it is at the discretion of your plan. After 2001, amounts between $1,000 and $5,000 may be automatically rolled over into an IRA designated by your plan. Check with your plan.
- *Fewer plan advantages.* While you will continue to make earnings on investments left in your plan, you are no longer an

employee and, therefore, no longer be able to make contributions or earn an employee match.

Individual Retirement Account (IRA)

If you can't leave your money in your former plan and must wait to participate in your new employer's plan, you can roll your money directly into an IRA. In this tax-free shelter, your money can continue growing and give you the option of transfer to your new employer's 401(k) when you are ready. You also have the option of splitting your 401(k) assets between an IRA and a 401(k) plan (from either your new or previous employer). As discussed in Chapter 17, IRAs face the same 10 percent early withdrawal federal income tax penalty if you take money out of the plan before age $59\frac{1}{2}$. (Note: Termination distributions from a 401(k) plan are not subject to the 10 percent early withdrawal federal income tax penalty if taken after the age of 55.) Unlike a 401(k), however, you may withdraw IRA funds without extra taxation in certain circumstances, such as for the purchase of a primary residence or for the payment of college expenses for a family member.

If you want to roll over your assets into an IRA, you must keep four things in mind:

1. *You set up the IRA.* It is up to you to research the financial firms and institutions offering IRAs and make sure your IRA is set up in a timely manner.
2. *Traditional IRAs only.* Only a traditional, deductible IRA is acceptable for rollovers. You may not roll over your account into a Roth IRA, a SIMPLE IRA, or a Coverdell Education Savings Account (formerly known as an Education IRA).
3. *Make it direct.* Never let your plan administrator hand you a check with only your name on it; it should also include the name of your IRA administrator as well. Your assets should be moved directly into an IRA or you are in essence taking a distribution, which means paying the 20 percent withholding tax as well as the 10 percent early withdrawal federal income tax penalty if you are younger than age $59\frac{1}{2}$.

4. *Don't make contributions.* Prior to 2002, if you rolled your 401(k) assets into an IRA, any additional contributions to this IRA would make the money ineligible for later transfer to a new 401(k) plan. While this is no longer the law, many plans still follow this practice. If you hope to roll your IRA account into a new employer's 401(k) plan at a later date, maintain two IRAs—one for your rollover and one for your IRA contributions.

Taking a Distribution

If you take a distribution, whether it be on purpose or accidentally because you missed the 30-day deadline, you will receive the assets from your account in a lump-sum, minus a 20 percent federal withholding tax.

For example, the amount in your account was $1,000 and you received a distribution of $800. When you receive your money you will have three choices:

1. *You can spend the $800.* In this case, you will owe federal and state income taxes, and the 10 percent early withdrawal tax penalty on the entire $1,000. The amount you owe in federal tax will be offset by the $200 that was withheld.
2. *You can roll over $800.* You have 60 days from the date of distribution to change your mind and roll over your $800 into an IRA or another eligible employer-offered plan. In this case, you will owe federal and state income taxes, and the 10 percent early withdrawal tax penalty on $200 that was withheld. This amount is still considered a distribution. However, the amount you owe in federal tax will be reduced by the $200 withheld.
3. *You can roll over $1,000.* You have the same 60 days to roll over the entire amount of your distribution, if you can make up the withheld $200 out of your own pocket. In this case, you will owe no tax or early withdrawal tax penalty, and the withheld $200 will be used to offset other federal income taxes for that year.

It is critical that you fill out the paperwork for a rollover well before the 30-day deadline expires if you want to keep your entire 401(k) account tax-sheltered.

Special Considerations

Young Employees

Early on in your career, you may not plan to stay long at a company, or even in that particular field of work. In fact, as a young employee first entering the work force you might change jobs every two or three years until you find a position in which you wish to stay. Thanks to portability, you can always keep your money working for you, no matter where you work. Do not allow uncertainties about your current job to keep you from participating in your employer's 401(k) plan.

Year-End Contributions

If employer matching or profit sharing contributions are made at year-end for everyone employed through December 31st, don't quit December 23rd and miss the entire year's employer contribution.

Pay Off Your Loans

As discussed in Chapter 5, if you have a loan at the time your employment ends, your loan may come due. If so, you may be given a limited amount of time to repay the loan, and if you are unable to repay it, your loan will be considered in default. When this occurs, the nonpayment of the loan is reported to the federal government and the amount in default is considered a hardship withdrawal. This means that you will face regular taxes plus the 10 percent hardship withdrawal penalty if you are less than $59^{1}/_{2}$ years old.

Vesting

Try to be fully vested in your plan assets before you leave for a new job. While you always own your own contributions and earnings on those amounts, if you are not 100 percent vested at the time your employment ends, you will not own all of the employer matching contributions and earnings.

You're 25

Start Saving Now

In a poll, Americans in their 20s and 30s said they had more confidence in the existence of UFOs than in the long-term viability of Social Security. And according to Fidelity Investments, 50 percent of employees in their 20s are saving in their company's 401(k) plan, as are 46 percent of American workers making between $10,000 and $20,000. Today's 20- and 30-year-old workers understand the need to start saving for retirement early—which is remarkable, because such saving behavior was unheard of in earlier generations.

But what if you are among today's youngest workers and you still haven't started saving and investing for retirement? Many employees in their 20s, trying to adjust to being financially independent after college, feel they can barely pay their bills, much less save for a retirement 40 years into the future. Debt from school loans, the seemingly easy access of money through credit cards, and the idea that twenty-somethings are "just too young" to save are among the reasons why younger workers do not participate. But the real issue is that you may not realize that the best time to save in your 401(k) plan is now.

The Benefits of Saving Early

Does retirement seem far away? The path towards a successful retirement is just like the saying "the journey of a thousand miles begins with a single step." And what a step! Anything you save when you are young lets you leap ahead on the road toward retirement security. Every dollar you contribute now is three you will not have to save later. Once you start saving and see that account balance grow, it will be easier to continue. So the earlier you begin, the better.

Maybe you can't imagine yourself as old and retired? The fact that retirement is not yet on your radar screen does not mean that you should not be saving. In fact, because you do not have the pressure of an approaching retirement and are not yet worried about having enough, it is the perfect time to save. Just remember that every dollar you put aside now cuts your hassle and worry, as well as how much you must save ten years down the line.

Does saving seem impossible right now? You may be overwhelmed with first-time financial woes, but keep in mind that this period will pass—and the years will bring other obligations. Starting to save for retirement now will actually be easier than when you are worrying about a mortgage, raising a family, or saving for college for your children. Chances are, you also have the advantage of good health, which could become a financial issue in the future. Unforeseen financial needs may show up down life's road, so you have a definite advantage by starting now when your responsibilities and financial commitments are limited.

Even so, is saving still low on your list? Is it hard to budget for retirement saving? Is it always the last thing on your list? Try payroll deduction, which automatically deducts the money from your paycheck before taxes. If you don't have to make a conscious decision about saving, it will become an unconscious habit. Plus you don't miss what you don't have. After a few months, you'll simply get used to having a little bit less.

Perhaps you're worried that you might need your money in a few years? If you don't like the idea of locking away part of your paycheck for decades, consider that you have access to your money if you need it. Thanks to the loan feature offered by many plans, you can quickly and easily access your money. If your plan allows you access to your account by computer or telephone, you could get a loan in a matter of days. However, remember that your 401(k) plan is not like a bank account, so you should not take money out for everyday expenses. Only in the case of an emergency or a big life event, such as the purchase of a house, should you take money out of your 401(k). There is no need to deplete your retirement fund unnecessarily and you still have access to your money when it really counts.

The Power of Compounding

Still not convinced? You may think that the decades you have before retirement give you plenty of time to save, but if you wait, you may miss years of compounding and employer matching contributions. The earlier you start saving, the more you will have at retirement. For example, if you start saving 6 percent of a $25,000 paycheck at age 22, earning a 3 percent match from your employer and an 8 percent rate of return, you may have more than $1 million by retirement. But by waiting only one year to start saving, you would have nearly $100,000 less at retirement. Just think, saving $1,500 now may mean $100,000 later.

Here's another example. Who will have more money: Pat, who saves $2,000 per year at age 25, 26, and 27 and then stops; or Gerry, who starts saving $2,000 per year at age 45 and continues to save until she retires 20 years later? Because Pat started early, an 8 percent return combined with the power of compounding will provide him with $120,915 at age 65—after an initial investment of only $6,000. Gerry would have only $95,114 at age 65, after contributions that total $40,000. If you save the money early, the compounding of your assets pays you so much more.

Also keep in mind that the suggested contribution amount—for example, 6 percent of your paycheck or $1,500—is not a tremendous amount, especially because it's pretax. By giving up a little now—for example, the latest CD, a new pair of shoes, or one night out a month—you will receive a tremendous retirement. Even if you can only start small, start saving now. If you put the loose change you pick up every day in your 401(k), it could buy you a new car when you retire.

14

You're 50
Prepare for Retirement

We have already discussed the importance of periodic changes in your asset allocation—such as rebalancing every year to compensate for shifts in your asset allocation and adjusting your allocation after major life changes alter your retirement goal. But you must also consider that you will have different asset allocation needs at different times in your life.

Managing your retirement investments has three phases:

1. *Accumulation.* This occurs from when you begin to work until five to ten yeas from retirement. In this phase, you save and invest to build financial wealth from which you will draw retirement income. Because you are further away from retirement, you can invest aggressively.
2. *Transition.* This period includes your working years five to ten years prior to retirement. In this phase, you transition your account balances from a more aggressive accumulation allocation to an investment allocation more appropriate for taking retirement distributions.
3. *Distribution.* This occurs from retirement onward. In this phase, you are withdrawing money from your investments, which reduces the principle. You need to rethink your investment approach and include investments that will provide a steady stream of income.

Transition Investing

In the market correction of 2001, the retirement prospects of most 401(k) participants were not affected. Because 401(k) assets are invested for the long term, a downturn merely gave these participants an opportunity to purchase stocks at lower prices. However, there was a small group of 401(k) participants who were financially injured: those who were planning to retire in 2001 or 2002, and had their 401(k) money aggressively invested. Unfortunately, they were unable to move their investments to a more appropriate approach before the stock market values declined.

Fluctuation in the stock market is a normal part of equity investing, but if you remain aggressively invested close to retirement, it could have serious consequences. The participants described above should have begun altering their investment strategy at least two years prior, and ideally five years prior, to their retirement so that they would not be exposed to this market volatility. For those who took a serious hit, the market shift forced a delayed retirement date or a lower standard of living in retirement. This is the consequence of poor planning, excessive optimism, and lack of education—one you should never have to face.

Ideally, you will give yourself a five-year window to gradually alter your investments. This will allow you to keep your portfolio balanced and give you time to adjust your investment strategy as needed. The youngest you can retire and avoid early retirement penalties is 55 years of age, so at age 50 you should at least begin planning how to transition your investment approach away from an accumulation strategy. Whether you decide to retire at 55 years old or 75 years old, this is the perfect time to prepare.

Your first step is determining what your new asset allocation should be. Reducing your risk does not mean taking all of your money out of stocks. Stocks continue to provide the best return over the long term. Instead, you could move your money from aggressive stock funds to more moderate or conservative stock fund choices.

Make a New Plan

Some people think that investing ends at retirement. If you take all of your money out in a lump-sum distribution and put it into a savings account or a "safe" low-return CD, then it does. Case closed. But that would undermine all the hard work you have done and drastically reduce your funds in retirement. Why? You will probably live for another 20 years (if not more), in which case you want your money to continue earning interest to increase your assets and beat inflation. If you do not need your money all at once at retirement, you can make periodic withdrawals from your retirement savings to provide you with income, while the rest of your assets remain money-generating investments.

You should start developing a plan for managing your investments in retirement at least five years before your planned retirement date—basically, at the same time that you will be phasing out of your aggressive accumulation approach. When you are making your retirement investment plan, you have to consider two new issues:

1. *You will be taking money out permanently.* When you take distributions you are reducing your interest-building money, or principle. This means you must choose which investments to remove the money from, as this could affect your asset allocation. To preserve your asset allocation mix, you can withdraw money proportionately from all investments. For example, let's assume you are invested 50 percent in stock funds and 50 percent in money market funds. If you need to withdraw $1,000, you would take $500 from the stock funds and $500 from your money market funds.
2. *You will be managing risk differently.* You need to continue investing in stocks, which means thinking five or ten years down the road. At the same time, you must balance that with your immediate needs for annual income, which means putting some of your money in lower-return but safer investments.

Over your years as an investor, you may have adjusted your asset allocation slowly according to your age and any major changes that took place in your life. You may have also periodically rebalanced your money when certain funds grew larger or smaller than their intended percentage. You can draw on those experiences to guide you now as you reallocate your account.

Keep in mind that every time you take a distribution, you must rebalance your money to make sure it spreads out evenly in the percentages you desire. Also, every few years you must alter those percentages, adapting your portfolio more and more for the short term. One possible way to handle this change is to move the money you intend to take as a distribution every six months into a secure interest-paying investment, such as a stable value or money market fund. Because these are excellent investments for the periods less than two years, they are a good choice for holding assets that will be withdrawn. Every six months when you take your distribution, you can move next year's money into the money market fund from your stocks and bonds, making sure to keep the percentages balanced according to your allocation plan. As you can see, it is not the *amount* of money in each kind of investment that you control when you rebalance; it is the percentage of your overall money in each investment.

You will make adjustments to your allocation percentages each year, slowly moving some of your investments out of more aggressive funds. By the time ten years has elapsed, your 401(k) will be invested in a way that will let you take distributions while minimizing short-term volatility risk.

If your retirement timeline will be relatively short—for example, if you retire later in life or if you expect to have a shorter-than-average life span—you should be reducing your more aggressive investments more quickly. Because your expected length of investment is shorter, you will have less time to recover from the market should a large drop occur.

Catch-Up Contributions

If you are age 50 or older within the end of the plan year, your plan may permit you to make catch-up contributions that exceed the regular 401(k) contribution limits. In 2002, you will be able to make a catch-up contribution of up to $1,000, and the amount you can contribute will be increased each year thereafter. Figure 14.1 details the contribution amounts for the coming years.

Please note that your employer is not required to allow catch-up contributions. But if you are over 50 years old and your company does offer you the option of these extra contributions, please do so! If you want to save even more, you can also put money into an IRA, though, depending on your income, your contributions may not be deductible.

Planning Your Estate

By the time you are in your 50s, you should at least have a will. Likewise, it would be beneficial to have a lawyer prepare other legal documents such as power of attorney or a living trust. If the prospect of dealing with a lawyer does not appeal to you, consider this: When dealing with the legal inheritance of your retirement plan, you'll need no lawyers, only the proper paperwork. 401(k) plans and other retirement vehicles are governed by inheritance rules that are separate from your will and in the event of your death, it is your beneficiary who will receive your funds.

There's more good news: When you name a beneficiary, your designation does not go through probate to prove the validity of your choice as with a will. This means that your 401(k) money is not subjected to the taxes and delays that an inheritance would

---

FIGURE 14.1   Catch-Up Contribution Increases for Participants Age 50 or Older

	Catch-Up Amount	*Total Permitted*
2002	$1,000	$12,000
2003	$2,000	$14,000
2004	$3,000	$16,000
2005	$4,000	$18,000
2006	$5,000	$20,000

After 2006, contributions will be indexed to inflation by $500 increments every year thereafter.

---

face. If you fail to make a will, your 401(k) money will still go directly to the beneficiary while the rest of your estate is divided up by the state. Just a reminder: Your spouse is your beneficiary unless your spouse agrees otherwise.

However, if you fail to designate your beneficiary, your 401(k) money will pass to your estate. The funds will then be distributed among your heirs if you have a will, or divided up by the state if you have no will. This could lead to complications such as extra taxes and improper dispersal of your money (you gave Uncle Earl your best fishing pole in your will, but did you really want to give him your money as well?). Keep in mind that anyone receiving your 401(k) funds will have to pay income tax on the money if they receive it as a distribution, so the kindest way to leave behind this gift is with as few additional taxes as possible.

It's Never Too Late

If you are 40, 45, or even 50 years old and have not yet begun saving for retirement, don't despair! Many people focus on raising a family and paying for day-to-day expenses, only to start investing when the kids are out of the house. The key is that you *do* start to save, rather than giving up. No matter what your age, it is never too late to start saving.

In fact, your situation is remarkably better than you imagine. Starting at age 40, if you set aside $600 dollars a month and receive a 12 percent rate of return, you could be a millionaire by the time you are 65. Creating a retirement nest egg of that size in so short a time requires two variables: putting aside enough money and getting the best rate of return.

Putting Aside Enough Money

It is true that to make up for lost time you will need to contribute more every month than if you had begun contributing in your 20s. However, one of the advantages to starting later in life is that you are most likely making more money now. From age 40 until your retirement, you are in your peak earning years, and once your kids are out of the house you really will have extra money in the bank.

If you simply cannot save enough now to meet your retirement goal, consider the following suggestions:

- Sell your home and purchase a residence with a lower mortgage payment.
- Use your home as a rental property.
- Retire and then go back to work at a later date.
- Sell your second car.
- Cut back on costly habits such as eating at fancy restaurants and taking expensive vacations.

Getting the Best Rate of Return

At this stage of the game, you cannot put all of your money into a stable value fund or professionally managed account and expect to make enough. These conservative funds are designed for investors who want a hands-off approach to their retirement fund and have lots of time to allow their money to grow. Unfortunately, you do not have the time to be so laid-back. Plus, you really need to be fully focused on your goal. This will require research to fully understand your plan's options and their rates of return, keeping an eye on your investments, and even discussing your choices with an investment professional.

If you do not already use the Internet and your company's automatic phone system, start doing so immediately. There is no better and quicker source for information about how your plan is doing than via these technologies. If you have decided that you are too old to learn how to use the Internet, I have some good news for you: You *can* still learn, no matter what your age. Start by taking a class or having your children sit down to work with you. Even better, have your grandchildren explain a few things (having grown up with computers, technology is a natural part of their lives).

However you approach your goal to become computer-literate, definitely be patient with yourself. No matter how frustrating it gets, remember that you are doing this for a very important cause—your retirement future.

401(k) at Retirement

15

You have followed your long-term plan. You have saved enough, invested for growth, and rebalanced every year. After participating in the 401(k) system during your working years, you are ready to retire and enjoy your golden years. Now what do you do? Today, you have several financial options:

- Keep your money in your 401(k) plan
- Roll the money into an IRA
- Buy an annuity
- Take a lump-sum distribution
- A combination of these options

Keep in mind that if you have retired, on April 1st of the year following the year you reach age $70^{1}/_{2}$, you *must* begin taking distributions of your 401(k) savings and paying taxes on it to the IRS. In fact, after age $70^{1}/_{2}$ you must take a minimum amount out of your plan every year, as calculated by the IRS. If you do not, you will end up paying a hefty fine. (See the end of this chapter for more information.)

Keeping Your Money in Your 401(k) Plan

In the past, you would have been expected to take your retirement distribution and manage the money on your own. However, plan sponsors are now looking past the final deadline of retirement and many will allow you to keep your money in the plan.

A number of possible pitfalls await plan participants who are not ready to handle a large retirement distribution: uninformed choices, self-serving brokers and financial planners, even neglect. But within your company's 401(k) plan, you are on familiar ground.

Possible benefits of keeping your retirement assets in your plan include:

- Familiarity with the plan, its options and administration
- Distribution flexibility
- Secure management
- Prescreened investment options
- The availability of a stable value fund
- Plan loans
- Paperwork to remind you of your plan-related decisions
- Lower fees
- Protection from creditors

Offering you this option is beneficial for your company as well. Retaining retirement balances in the 401(k) plan permits your employer to negotiate lower fees and beneficial service arrangements for all of its plan participants.

If you decide to leave your money with your employer when you retire, do not assume that everything will remain the same. Take the time to learn how the plan works for retirees, and always stay in close contact with your plan, especially keeping your company informed of any changes in address. Also, if you have special needs, be sure to communicate them to your company's human resources department.

Lump-Sum Distributions

Taking a lump-sum distribution means receiving a check for the full amount in your account. The money is yours to invest, spend, or save as you please. However, when considering a lump-sum distribution, keep the following in mind:

- *You will be immediately taxed on the entire amount.* This could result in your entire distribution being taxed at the highest income tax rate. In contrast, if you keep your distribution in a tax-sheltered plan and take withdrawals in installment payments, you will pay tax on only the amount you withdraw. By paying taxes in smaller increments further down the line, you could end up paying less as your tax bracket drops.

- *Once you have your money in your hands, the temptation to spend it will be great.* If you don't need your money for a substantial expense, like the purchase of a retirement home, it is much safer to keep most of it in some kind of tax-sheltered retirement vehicle. That way you will not be tempted to spend your savings on unnecessary items.
- *You will need this money throughout your retirement.* You will not only need this money in 5 years, but also 15 years from now. To beat inflation and retain your purchasing power, you should keep your money invested and earning tax-deferred returns for as long as possible.

IRA Rollovers

One way to keep your retirement savings tax deferred after you retire is to roll your money over into an IRA. IRAs and 401(k) plans are similar in that you can choose when and how much to withdraw after you retire, at least until you reach age 70½, when you must begin taking the legally required minimum distributions.

Rolling 401(k) retirement savings into an IRA is a popular choice with many participants. On one hand, by choosing to place the money in another tax-sheltered plan, you have all the benefits of your former plan, including tax-deferred earnings on your investments, security, and structure. On the other hand, you have much more freedom with investment choices in an IRA, such as the ability to take money out whenever you want and the option to continue contributing money to your account. However, with that flexibility comes additional responsibility for managing your investments and making withdrawal decisions.

If you decide to take a lump-sum distribution and later change your mind, you have 60 days to roll the money into an IRA. But doing so can be tricky. Because you took a lump-sum distribution, the IRS took 20 percent towards taxes just in case. Don't worry, if you do roll over the funds you will get all that back later. However, for the time being, you have 20 percent fewer funds to roll over. If you want to roll over 100 percent of your original amount, just be prepared with cash in hand to make up for that missing 20 percent.

Annuities

A tax-deferred annuity is a contract that you purchase from an insurance company. You give the company money in advance and the company agrees to pay you, usually monthly, a fixed amount of income for a set period or for the rest of your life. Converting your retirement savings to fixed payments by purchasing an annuity is a good approach if you want security and do not want to be responsible for the ongoing management of your retirement savings.

However, whatever savings you convert into an annuity cannot be withdrawn or taken as a loan. Your may only receive distributions according to the schedule in your annuity agreement. Also, the purchasing power of fixed monthly payments will be eroded over time by inflation. Plan to have some money set aside for emergencies, unexpected expenses, and to maintain the purchasing power of your monthly payments. Finally, be sure to understand the characteristics of any annuity contract you are considering. These would include the guarantees and the fixed rate or variable investment options. In addition, many annuities have significant fees. Be sure to contact several companies for competing bids before you purchase any annuity.

If you leave your money in your 401(k) plan, you may be able to get the benefit of an annuity (i.e., fixed monthly payments) without losing control of your money or paying high fees. You do this by taking what are called installment payments. Companies that let you manage your retirement savings in their 401(k) plan may permit you to identify a fixed monthly payment schedule for distribution of your retirement money. They will also allow participants to change their withdrawal schedules, typically annually.

A Combination of Options

As an alternative, you can arrange for a combination of these options. For example, you can use a portion of your money to purchase monthly payments in the form of an annuity, and keep the rest of your assets in a tax-sheltered account that continues to make investment earnings. Your target goal for retirement was to have ten times final pay in your account. You could use 70 percent of that amount for installment payments or to purchase an annuity and keep 30 percent invested. This way you will continue earning on a portion of your assets to maintain your purchasing power and beat inflation, while still providing yourself with a fixed amount of money to live on. Keeping a portion of the money in a tax-sheltered account also gives you access to a portion of your money in case of emergencies.

Some financial planners suggest that you keep three years worth of expenses in cash investments after retirement. If you purchase an annuity as well as investing some of your money, you need only put into cash investments the amount you will need for those three years, minus what the annuity will pay you. This helps ensure that you will not be forced to take distributions from your investment in stock funds if the market is down.

Minimum Distributions at 70½

After retirement you might go back to work, you might have an inheritance to rely on, or you might even win the lottery. Whatever the case, on April 1st of the year following the year after you turn 70½ years old, you *must* begin taking money out of your account and paying taxes on it. In fact, the IRS calculates a minimum distribution for you based on your life expectancy. Every year that you live after that point, you must at least withdraw the minimum amount.

If you do not start taking out money as required, you could face a tax of 50 percent on the minimum distribution you should have taken. It can be shocking, especially after all the penalties you were warned about for taking money out too early, to discover even bigger penalties for waiting too long. But remember that you have been receiving a tax benefit on these funds for years. The IRS wants to encourage the creation of retirement funds with those pretax contributions, but not let it go on too long.

There is one way to postpone minimum distributions. If you never retired and are still working for the company that is housing your retirement funds, you may keep them in that plan. But the moment you stop working there after age $70^1/_2$, you must begin taking money out of the plan.

Professional Assistance

Administering your 401(k) savings after you retire requires planning and attentive management. Seeking the professional counsel of a financial advisor can be beneficial at any point in your 401(k) planning process, but this is especially true as you plan your retirement. Not only do you need to plan for a stream of payments to meet your monthly needs, you will have complicated tax, insurance, and estate planning decisions. A financial advisor can assist you with the complicated financial decisions that retirement planning will require. See Chapter 16, "Picking a Financial Advisor," for more on this subject.

16

Picking a Financial Advisor

Seeking the professional counsel of a financial advisor can be beneficial at any point in your 401(k) planning process. For example, a financial advisor can provide the support you need when you begin participating and want to fully take advantage of your investment options, or if a major change in your personal finances occurs and you need to rethink your retirement planning.

However, there is one particular time when everyone should consider the aid of a financial planner: when retirement approaches. As Chapter 14 discusses, a major review of your investment approach should take place approximately five years before you retire. A financial advisor can help you determine when you will need to start taking distributions from your 401(k), and when and how to transition from an aggressive accumulation approach to an investment allocation more appropriate for generating distributions. A financial advisor can also assist you with the other complicated financial decisions that retirement planning will require.

When you decide to work with a financial advisor, be prepared to interview several candidates to find the one who is right for you. Because your financial needs and goals are unique, you will be seeking a financial advisor whose methods, experience, and knowledge match your requirements.

You also need to pick a financial advisor with the right financial emphasis. There are financial planners available who can assist you on a number of issues other than retirement—including your taxes, saving for the purchase of a home, or regular investing. For that reason, it is important that the planner you choose knows that you are a 401(k) investor.

In addition, until you near retirement, your 401(k) investing should be based on a long-term investment strategy appropriate for you. You should not be making changes to that mix, except periodically to rebalance your account. If a financial planner tries to steer you towards a different approach, especially one that involves playing the market, keep looking. Be especially cautious when choosing a financial advisor if your 401(k) plan has a brokerage window, which allows you to pick investments that were not prescreened by your employer.

Finally, it is important when picking a financial advisor to find one who will deal openly and honestly with you and your money. The financial world involves the handling of large sums of money, which would be a temptation for anyone. Fortunately, the business of working with other people's assets is the most regulated business in the country, keeping the majority of planners ethical. If you keep your money in your 401(k) plan at retirement, which any good financial planner will advise you to do, you have the advantage of the protection provided by your employer's oversight of the plan.

While most financial planners are honest, you may encounter a financial advisor who has given in to financial pressures to generate income for his or her firm. According to *Brokerage Fraud: What Wall Street Doesn't Want You to Know,* by Tracy Pride Stoneman and Douglas Schulz (Dearborn 2001), some companies in the financial industry employ practices that tempt planners to bend the rules. An example of such a practice occurs when planners encourage you to constantly trade because it earns the firm commissions (this practice is called churning).

Employers often arrange for qualified financial planners to assist their retirees. The employer may pay the entire fee or negotiate a discounted rate. Remember that a license is no safeguard against churning, mark up of prices, unnecessary fees, promotion of stocks that involve a kickback, or other unlawful practices. Your best bet is to interview each candidate carefully to determine the kind of firm they work for, their expertise, and their honesty. In order to assist you with the process of selecting a financial planner, following are a number of questions for you to consider asking.

Are They Qualified?

All the financial planners you consider should be qualified. If you are not convinced that someone has the necessary expertise, drop them from your list immediately. To determine if someone is qualified, consider their:

- *Years of experience.* Look for someone with a minimum of three years experience giving advice.
- *Types of experience.* Your planner should be knowledgeable in investments, retirement planning, and retirement-related taxes.
- *Education and designations.* Someone with training and an appropriate financial planning designation (such as the Certified Financial Planner mark) is preferable. At the very least, planners must be registered with state or federal authorities.
- *Proven success.* Get a list of references and talk to each of them personally.

How Much Will They Cost?

A financial planner should always offer you an estimate on what services they will provide and how much these services will cost. In addition, they should give you a detailed list of all the costs you could incur, including:

- *General fees.* These may be based on a percentage of your assets, an hourly rate, or a flat rate. Your financial advisor may also charge you an annual maintenance fee in addition to other fees.
- *Commissions.* If applicable, these are usually a percentage of the amount you invest in a product. Some planners will reduce their other fees if they receive a commission.

Also be sure to find out from prospective financial planners whether they receive a salary from their company and/or if their income is based in some way on the assets they manage.

Are They Right for You?

Every planner offers different kinds of advice, and provides advice in a different style. Some questions to ask to determine differences in advice and style include:

- Will you be working with this financial planner one on one, or will an associate handle future planning sessions? Some financial planners also work with specialists in various fields to gain the benefit of their information. You may welcome the added input, or prefer to work only with one person.
- Does your financial planner favor a cautious style of investing, an aggressive one, or is he or she influenced primarily by your goals?
- Does your financial planner want to get an overview of your financial situation to provide a comprehensive approach, or are they focused specifically on your retirement needs only? Which approach do you prefer?

There is no format for picking the personality of a financial planner, because your financial planner's personal style must match your own distinctive learning style in a way that makes you feel comfortable. However, remember that the most personable financial planners are not necessarily the best. Their credentials and expertise must be as impressive as their manner is friendly or charming.

Who Else Benefits?

Like a car salesperson on commission, financial planners may have business relationships that will influence the choices they offer or suggestions they make. Your financial planner should volunteer this information and be willing to work with other choices if you prefer. However, certain relationships—for example, if your planner receives extra compensation based on selling certain products—are more problematic than others. Partnerships that influence your financial planner include:

- A business affiliation with any company whose products or services they recommend
- Receiving compensation based on selling products or services
- Referring you to other professionals, who provide the planner with compensation or other benefits
- A business affiliation with a broker or dealer
- Ownership or partial ownership of a company whose products are recommended

Get It in Writing

At the beginning of your work together, your financial planner should give you a packet of information that provides the details of his or her practice—including your financial planner's qualifications, the services offered, fees, and involvement in any business partnerships. If this information is not offered, or a packet of particular facts is not presented, you have the right to request that information. At the beginning of your work together, you should also request a written agreement of the services that will be provided to you.

In addition, your financial planner must be able to provide you with a disclosure form called Form ADV, or the state equivalent of that form. This form is a record of the planner's practice and will describe any unlawful or unethical actions he or she has taken. All financial planners who have registered as investment advisors with the Securities and Exchange Commission or state securities agencies, or who are associated with a company that is registered as an investment advisor, have a Form ADV on file.

For More Information

A number of national associations provide information that will be valuable to you as you pick a financial advisor.

To find a financial planner in your area, contact these sources:

- Certified Financial Planner Board of Standards
  888-CFP-MARK (888-237-6275)

- Financial Planning Association
  800-282-PLAN (800-282-7526)
- National Association of Personal Financial Advisors
  888-FEE-ONLY (888-333-6659)

To check the disciplinary history of a financial planner or advisor, contact the following:

- Certified Financial Planner Board of Standards
  888-CFP-MARK (888-237-6275)
- Securities and Exchange Commission
  800-732-0330

17

Other Plans
Differences and Similarities

401(k) plans are just one of the many types of retirement programs. Some of these programs are defined contribution plans, which, like a 401(k), allow you to postpone taxes on your contributions and earnings until your funds are withdrawn. In some cases, you may be able to participate in both a 401(k) and another retirement plan at the same time. Understanding the different types of retirement plans for which you are eligible will allow you to most effectively coordinate your retirement savings strategy.

Being able to identify the various types of retirement plans is also important. You need to continue meeting your retirement planning goals even if you cannot participant in a 401(k) plan.

Savings Plans Similar to a 401(k)

Every employer can provide its employees with a 401(k)-like plan, which allows participants to postpone taxes on contributions until the funds are withdrawn. However, these plans have different names depending on the type of employer.

- *457.* These are used by local and state governments, and by some nonprofit organizations.
- *403(b).* These are used by nonprofit, tax-exempt organizations such as schools, hospitals, or churches.
- *401(k).* These are used by all other employers, including most nonprofits.

You can also save on a pretax basis in an IRA. In some cases, an employer will sponsor an IRA program for its employees. But if no employer-sponsored IRA exists, you can still take advantage of an IRA through a bank or investment firm.

Some companies also offer nonqualified deferred compensation plans in addition to their 401(k). Such plans are usually available only to highly compensated employees.

457 Plans

457 plans are 401(k)-like plans offered by state and local governments, and some tax-exempt entities. Like a 401(k), participants in a 457 plan can save a portion of their earnings on a pretax basis. Unlike a 401(k), money saved in a 457 cannot be accessed by participating employees until they actually leave their jobs or retire. Until that time, 457 plan assets belong to the plan sponsor but are held in a trust account set up in an employee's name.

As with 401(k) plans, in 2002 the annual pretax individual contribution limit for 457 plans became $11,000. This amount will increase by $1,000 a year for four years, reaching a $15,000 limit in 2006. Further increases will be indexed to inflation. However, additional contributions can be made to 457 plans to make up for the lack of savings during your early years of employment. These catch-up contributions can be made in the three years preceding the normal retirement age, as defined by your plan.

In 2002, those eligible for a 457 catch-up contribution can save up to $22,000 (the $11,000 regular contribution plus an $11,000 catch-up). The maximum catch-up contribution will increase in $2,000 increments until it reaches $30,000 in 2006. As described elsewhere in this book, 401(k) plan participants over age 50 are also eligible to make catch-up contributions. If you are over age 50, you can contribute up to $1,000 more than the $11,000 401(k) limit for 2002. The 401(k) catch-up contribution limit will increase by $1,000 each year until 2006, when it will reach $5,000. 457 plan participants with a 401(k) are also eligible to make the 401(k) catch-up contribution— until they are within three years of retirement, at which time they are eligible to make the 457 catch-up contributions only.

Like 401(k) participants, employees participating in a govern-ment-provided 457 plan (but not one offered by a tax-exempt en-tity) may roll their assets over into a new employer's plan or into an IRA. Unlike a 401(k), employees who take a preretirement cash distribution at the end of employment are not subject to a 10 per-cent early withdrawal federal income tax penalty (paying only reg-ular income tax). However, if that money is rolled over into an IRA or a non-457 qualified retirement plan, the assets are reclassified and are subject to the 10 percent early withdrawal federal income tax penalty if withdrawn before age 59$^1/_2$.

In addition, state and local governments can permit workers with savings in a 401(k) or IRA to roll their pretax contributions and earnings into their 457 plan. Finally, state and local govern-ments can give their employees the option of using their 457 sav-ings to purchase pension plan credits.

403(b) Plans

403(b) plans are 401(k)-like plans offered by nonprofit, tax-exempt organizations such as schools, hospitals, and churches. These plans permit employees to save a portion of their earnings pretax through payroll deduction. In contrast to a 401(k) plan, 403(b) plans are limited in the investment options they can offer participants. 403(b) sponsors can only offer annuities—either fixed or variable—or mutual funds. Also, the law establishing the 403(b) plan requires that participants be offered an annuity upon retirement. For this reason, 403(b) plans are often known as tax-sheltered annuities or tax-deferred annuities.

403(b) plans have a special catch-up contribution option. Par-ticipants may make an additional $3,000 contribution each year for five years if they have been working for the same employer for more than 15 years. However, 403(b) annual contribution limits are the same as those for 401(k) and 457 plans. The maximum individual pre-tax contribution of these three plans is $11,000 in 2002, an amount which will increase by $1,000 a year for four years until reaching $15,000 in 2006. Further increases will be indexed to inflation.

There are several rollover possibilities for 403(b) plans. 403(b) savings may be rolled into a new employer's plan, whether it offers a 401(k), 403(b), or 457 plan. 403(b) plans may also be rolled over into an IRA at the end of employment or retirement. Likewise, pre-tax IRA assets and earnings may be rolled over into a 403(b) plan.

Preretirement distributions for 403(b) plans, like those from 401(k) plans, are subject to the 10 percent early withdrawal federal income tax penalty, unless the distribution is paid out as a life annuity or in installments for life. Finally, like some 457 participants, 403(b) savers can use their assets to purchase pension plan credits.

Individual Retirement Accounts (IRAs)

The term individual retirement account (IRA) is used to describe several types of governmentally encouraged savings programs. IRAs are available through banks and financial firms, or may be offered by your employer. You may contribute to an IRA outside of your employer even if you are eligible for a retirement plan where you work. However, if you contribute to both a 401(k) and an IRA, your IRA contributions will be limited or not tax deductible, depending on the amount of your annual income.

All IRAs are like 401(k) plans in that they permit the compounding of tax-deferred earnings on investments. However, there are significant differences between an IRA and a 401(k)—most significantly, maximum contribution limits. For the typical IRA, the contribution limit for the years 2002 through 2004 is $3,000. The limit increases to $4,000 for 2005 through 2007, and then to $5,000 for 2008 and thereafter.

As with your 401(k), you can save more in your IRA when you are older than age 50. Additional IRA contributions for those over age 50 can be up to $500 in 2002, an amount which will increase to $1,000 for 2006 and thereafter.

The second major difference between IRAs and 401(k)s is that in most cases you must set up your own IRA, while your employer always sets up your 401(k) plan. This means selecting a bank, brokerage firm, insurance company, or mutual fund company from which to obtain your IRA. If you wish to set up an IRA, you will complete an application form at the financial company of your choice and determine how to invest the money in your account. If your IRA is tax deductible, it will be your responsibility to make sure you report your IRA contributions on your income tax forms and do not exceed the maximum contribution limits. In contrast, your tax-deferred 401(k) contributions are automatically accounted for on your employer-provided W-2 form, which reports your taxable income. In addition, your employer makes sure you do not exceed the legal contribution limits.

Deductible IRA. The most common form of IRA is one in which your contributions are deductible on your yearly income tax return. When you contribute, this reduces the amount of income tax you owe to the government. If you also participate in a retirement plan where you work, your IRA contributions may not be deductible or may be only partially deducible depending on your gross income. Figure 17.1 is a chart defining at what income level your contributions are fully deductible, partially deductible or not deductible at all.

The deductible IRA is designed to help you save for retirement, so if you withdraw funds from your IRA before age $59^1/_2$, in most cases you will face a 10 percent early withdrawal federal income tax penalty, plus regular income taxes. However, you may withdraw IRA funds without penalty before age $59^1/_2$ for the following reasons:

- To pay medical expenses that exceed 7.5 percent of income
- To pay for health insurance under certain circumstances

FIGURE 17.1   Income Phase-Out Range for Deductible Contributions

Year	Income Range for a Single Taxpayer	Income Range for Married Taxpayers Filing Jointly
2002	$40,000–$50,000	$60,000–$70,000
2003	$45,000–$55,000	$65,000–$75,000
2004	$50,000–$60,000	$70,000–$80,000
2005		$75,000–$85,000
2006		$80,000–$100,000

If your income is below the lowest number for the year, you may claim a full deduction. If your income falls within the phase-out range, you may claim a partial deduction. If you income is above the maximum, you cannot make deductible IRA contributions. Source: U.S. Congress.

- To pay the college expenses of you, your spouse, your children, or your grandchildren
- Up to $10,000 may be withdrawn to buy a house, after not owning one for at least two years

If you arrange for annual installment payments for the rest of your life, you can withdraw from your IRA without penalty at any time. At age $70^{1}/_{2}$, you can no longer make contributions to a deductible IRA and you must begin withdrawing at least the governmentally defined minimum amount.

Nondeductible IRA. A nondeductible IRA is the same as a deductible IRA, except for one important detail: none of the contributions you make can be deducted from your income for federal tax purposes. You can choose not to deduct your contributions and these funds will not be taxed when you withdraw them later. However, please note that your investment earnings within a nondeductible IRA are still tax-sheltered and will be taxed when you withdraw those funds. You may also withdraw your contributions, but not the earnings, without penalty at any time.

Roth IRA. Roth IRA is a version of the nondeductible IRA. Contributions to a Roth IRA are not tax deductible and are subject to the same maximum contribution limits as the traditional deductible IRA. However, earnings on Roth IRA investments are normally tax-free, unlike earnings on other nondeductible IRAs, which are taxed when withdrawn. In addition, you can only contribute to a Roth IRA if your income is less than the limit set by Congress.

Withdrawals from a Roth IRA are tax-free (including investment earnings) if your Roth IRA has existed for five years *and* if funds are withdrawn for the following reasons:

- To buy a house after not owning a house for at least two years (limited to $10,000)
- Because you have reached age $59^{1}/_{2}$
- Because you are disabled
- To be paid to your beneficiary because of your death

If a preretirement Roth IRA withdrawal is made for medical expenses, college expenses, or by annual lifetime payments, you will avoid the 10 percent early withdrawal income tax penalty. However, you will have to pay regular taxes on your investment earnings.

No minimum distribution must be taken from a Roth IRA at age $70^1/_2$, and you can continue contributing to the Roth IRA indefinitely. Also, if your income is below the amount set by Congress, you can convert a traditional deductible IRA to a Roth IRA by paying regular income tax on the amount converted.

Rollover and conduit IRAs. When you change jobs or retire, you are permitted to take the money from your employer's retirement plan and roll it over into an IRA. Prior to 2002, you were required to keep this rollover money in a conduit IRA, in which you would make no contributions if you wished to move the money eventually into a new employer's plan. When you rolled over money from your employer's retirement plan and made additional contributions, this was known as a rollover IRA. Now, there is no legal restriction to making contributions to such IRAs. However, in case a future employer will only accept an IRA rollover from a conduit IRA, you may want to continue holding your plan rollovers in a conduit IRA form.

Education IRA. The education IRA allows you—and anyone else who wishes to contribute—to save for your child's or grandchild's college education. Contributions are limited to $1,000 per year and are not deductible on your tax return. Once the child in question turns age 18, you can no longer make contributions. However, withdrawals are tax-free (including investment earnings) and penalty-free when used for college expenses. Money can be left in this plan until the child turns 30 years old, when it must be withdrawn and taxed. This penalty may be avoided, however, if the funds are moved to an education IRA for another family member.

Other Employer-Provided Retirement Plans

Congress has allowed for a number of employer-provided retirement programs in addition to 401(k), 457, and 403(b) plans. Some are tailored for self-employed individuals or very small businesses. All provide a tax-exemption for retirement savings, but require taxation upon distribution. With exceptions that parallel the 401(k) plan rules, preretirement distributions from these other retirement programs will result in a 10 percent federal income tax penalty.

Deferred Profit Sharing

A deferred profit sharing plan is an employer-provided, defined-contribution retirement plan designed to share company profits with employees, but on a tax-deferred basis. Company contributions may be determined by either a fixed formula or at the discretion of the board of directors. Benefits at retirement are the sum total of the contributions made plus investment earnings. A deferred profit sharing plan may be combined with a 401(k) plan so that participants can make tax-deferred contributions to the plan.

Traditional Pension Plans

If you are a participant in a traditional pension plan, also called a defined-benefit plan, your employer will pay you a monthly retirement benefit based on your length of service and salary. In some cases, at retirement you may be able to take as a distribution the lump sum value of your benefit instead of receiving monthly payments. In most cases, those who take a lump sum from a traditional pension plan roll it over into an IRA.

Money Purchase Plan

A money purchase plan is an employer-provided, defined-contribution retirement plan in which the employer's contributions are determined by a specific formula, usually as a percentage of pay. Benefits at retirement are the sum total of all contributions made plus investment earnings. Employer contributions in a money purchase plan are not dependent on company profits. Money purchase plans can be offered in addition to a 401(k) plan.

Target-Benefit Plan

A target-benefit plan is an employer-provided, defined-contribution retirement plan in which employer contributions are based on an actuarial valuation designed to provide a target benefit to each participant upon retirement. The plan does not guarantee that such benefit will be paid. Its obligation is to make targeted contributions. The benefit paid is whatever can be provided by the amount in the participant's account when the participant retires or terminates employment.

Cash Balance Plan

A cash balance plan is an employer-provided, defined-benefit plan. In a typical cash balance plan, a participant's account is credited each year with a pay credit (such as 5 percent of compensation from his or her employer) and an interest credit (either a fixed rate or a variable rate that is linked to an index such as the one-year Treasury bill rate). Increases and decreases in the value of the plan's investments do not directly affect the benefit amounts promised to participants. Thus, the investment risks and rewards on plan assets are felt only by the employer.

When a participant becomes entitled to receive benefits under a cash balance plan, the account balance can always be taken in the form of an annuity. In certain cash balance plans, however, the participant could instead choose to take a lump sum benefit equal to the account balance. The availability of this option is solely at the discretion of the employer.

Keogh Plan

A Keogh plan is a specialized retirement program in which a self-employed individual or member of a partnership can make contributions. These contributions are tax deductible to the business or partnership but not taxable to the individual until the money is withdrawn. A Keogh plan can use either a defined-contribution or defined-benefit format.

Simplified Employee Pension Plan (SEP)

In a simplified employee pension (SEP) plan, also known as a SEP/IRA, an employer makes retirement contributions into IRAs set up by an employee. Benefits at retirement are the sum total of all contributions made plus investment earnings. SEP plans are ruled by the following guidelines:

- The employee is immediately vested in the employer contributions.
- The employer contributions are not included in an employee's income.
- Once the employer contribution has been made into the IRA, IRA rules apply.

SIMPLE Plans

Savings Incentive Match Plans for Employees (SIMPLE) plans are designed for small companies with 100 or fewer employees. In a SIMPLE plan, you could contribute up to $7,000 in 2002. The maximum you can contribute will increase $1,000 a year until it reaches $10,000 in 2005. It will be indexed to inflation thereafter.

Companies using this program must match 100 percent of employee contributions up to 3 percent of compensation, or provide contributions up to 2 percent for all eligible employees, even if they are not contributing to the plan. These contributions are immediately and 100 percent vested, and they are the only employer contribution to the plan. Unlike similar retirement plans, there is a two-year waiting period before money in a SIMPLE plan can be withdrawn or transferred without a 25 percent penalty. SIMPLE plans may be structured as IRAs or as 401(k) plans.

401(k) and Military Leave

The Uniform Services Employment and Reemployment Act of 1994 (USERRA) provides employment related rights to the men and women who leave their jobs to serve their country. If you are eligible for USERRA, you may qualify for rights that include continued health care coverage during your leave, reemployment in a similar position at your employing company, and a reinstatement of retirement benefits after your return.

Eligibility under USERRA

You will be eligible for USERRA if you meet two requirements: providing service to your country as specified, and providing sufficient notice that you will be absent.

Service

In order to qualify for special rights under USERRA, you must be leaving work to perform *service*. This is defined as any of the following:

- Active duty
- Training for active or inactive duty
- Initial active duty
- Full-time National Guard duty
- Examinations to determine fitness for duty

Each of these definitions of service is valid whether your participation in the military is voluntary or involuntary. To be eligible for USERRA, you also must be called to duty or take a leave of absence to serve in one of the following capacities:

- Active duty U.S. armed services
- Reserves
- National Guard
- Coast Guard
- Commissioned corps of the public health services
- At the request of the president

Notice

You or an officer from the military branch you are serving must provide to your company advance notice of military leave. This notice may be verbal or in writing. If you fail to provide notice, you could be subject to the conduct rules and established policy of your company concerning unexcused absences. If notice is otherwise impossible or unreasonable due to military necessity, advance notice is not required. Furthermore, if you are called to serve your country by the president of the United States, you do not need to provide advance notice.

At the completion of your leave, you must also provide advance notice to your employer that you are ready to return to work. Following is the schedule for providing notice to your employer upon your return from military service:

- *If your service was less than 31 days,* at the end of service you have eight hours plus transportation time to report that you are ready to return to work.
- *If your service was between 31 and 180 days,* application for reemployment must be submitted no later than 14 days after end of the service.
- *If your service was more than 180 days,* application for reemployment must be submitted no later than 90 days after end of the service.

- *If you were hospitalized or convalescing,* you may be hospitalized or recovering from injury for up to two years and still be eligible for reemployment. However, after your recovery period, your application for reemployment must be submitted within the standard 90 days.

Ineligibility under USERRA

Please note that you are ineligible for reemployment rights under USERRA in the following situations:

- Your employment was terminated before you gave notice of your military leave.
- You were employed on a temporary basis for a brief, nonrecurrent period under which there was no reasonable expectation that employment would continue.
- A change in your employer's circumstance makes reemployment impossible (for example, a reduction in work force that would have included you).
- Your length of military service was longer than five years.
- You were dishonorably discharged or separated from the military for any other disqualifying reason.

Time Requirements

Five years of military service is the maximum length of time that you can be absent and remain eligible for reemployment under USERRA.

Pay during Your Absence

Providing notice may generate more benefits than are required under the law. Your employer has the option to pay you all or a portion of your wages during your absence, and will likely be more generous if you provide clear notice before and after your leave. If your employer does not pay you during your military service, you cannot be forced to use paid leave time during your absence. It is up to you whether to take that time as paid leave (for example, vacation or sick days) or unpaid leave.

401(k) Rights under USERRA

The law requires that you be promptly reemployed, which is left open to the good judgment and necessity of your employer. For example, if you have weekend National Guard duty or must be absent for one day for a military examination, your reinstatement should be immediate. But if your leave was five years in duration (the maximum length), your employer may have to give notice to the employee who worked in your position during your absence.

If you are eligible for reemployment under USERRA you are also eligible for special rights concerning your participation in your company's 401(k) plan. These rights include allowing you to make up the contributions you would have made to your 401(k) plan via salary reduction and receiving an employer match (if offered) on those contributions. Also:

- For vesting and benefit accrual purposes, you must be treated as though no break in employment took place.
- On your return you have the right to make missed contributions to the plan. The repayment period is three times the length of military service or five years, whichever is less.
- If your company offers an employer matching contribution, your plan must make up the matching contribution when you make your missed contributions to the plan. If the match is based on percent of pay, company contributions will be made according to the pay you would have received if you had not been on leave. If this rate is uncertain, the company contribution will be based on your average rate of compensation during the year prior to your military leave.
- Your plan may suspend loan repayments during military service, but is not required to do so.

- The law is unclear as to whether you can make 401(k) contributions to your plan from any pay you receive from your employer during your military leave.

Through the USERRA law, the government wishes to support the needs and goals of those who are a part of the United States military. If you leave your current employment to serve your country, you should be able to return to work, proceeding on your career path and continuing to build your retirement future.

401(k) and Divorce

In a divorce, your former spouse and any dependents may be entitled to a portion of your 401(k) assets. If this is the case, the court will issue a qualified domestic relations order (QDRO) as part of your divorce settlement to define the what, when, and how of the division of your account.

A QDRO is a court judgement, decree, or order that names someone other than you as a recipient of your 401(k) assets. This other person, known as the alternate payee, may only be your spouse, your former spouse, your child, or any other dependent. The QDRO is used in the division of assets in a divorce settlement for alimony payments, child support payments, or property rights payments. If you are involved in a divorce proceeding, be sure to ask your plan administrator if there is a model QDRO form for your plan. Doing so early on in the process will save you time and expense.

There is one piece of good news in this situation. The money removed from your account for a QDRO is not subject to the 10 percent early withdrawal federal income tax penalty—even if you and your alternate payee are both younger than age 59½. Unfortunately, if the QDRO is not properly established, you *will* be subject to the 10 percent early withdrawal federal income tax penalty. In the midst of divorce and the distribution of your account to other parties, the last thing you want to face is a tax on money that is no longer yours.

Ensuring the Validity of a QDRO

In order for a QDRO to be valid, it must meet two legal requirements: It must be correctly created and it must be correctly verified.

Checking the status of your QDRO at both stages is wise to ensure that your QDRO is acceptable under the law. If this seems like a lot of trouble, keep in mind that aside from preventing undo taxation, the other reason why such checking and double-checking takes place is to prevent someone from illegally accessing your 401(k) assets.

Creation of the QDRO

To be considered a QDRO, the division of your assets must first and foremost be issued by a court order in compliance with state laws. However, the QDRO must also include the following information to be valid:

- Your name and your last known mailing address
- The name and address of your alternate payee
- The amount or percentage of your account to be given to your alternate payee
- The manner in which the amount or percentage is to be determined
- The number of payments or period to which the order applies
- The plan to which the order applies

Verification of the QDRO

If your 401(k) plan is subject to a QDRO, you must provide your plan administrator with either the original court order or a court-certified copy of your QDRO document. Your plan administrator will then follow formal procedures to establish the legality of the QDRO and put it into motion. These procedures are part of the rules set down in your 401(k) summary plan description, and by law they must include:

- Notifying you and the alternate payee that the order was received, and detailing the procedures that will be followed to verify the order.

- Determining within a reasonable period of time (no longer than 18 months after the order is issued) whether the order is a valid QDRO.
- Accounting separately for any amounts payable to your alternate payee during the evaluation period.
- Notifying you and your alternate payee whether the QDRO is valid.

A QDRO Case Study

In a famous case, a man paid out $1 million dollars from his retirement plan as part of his divorce settlement. The man assumed that the order was a QDRO, but missed several key elements that caused the order to be invalid. First, the man's former wife was not identified as the alternate payee. Second, the order did not include the name or address of the alternate payee. Third, the man did not follow proper procedure for verifying the order.

Because the man was the administrator of the retirement plan in question, he argued that he did not need to file forms with himself, and that the order did not need to include the name and address of the alternate payee because he was personally aware of the details. The IRS did not agree, and deemed the settlement payment an early distribution and, therefore, subject to the 10 percent early withdrawal federal income tax penalty.

The Division of Funds in a Divorce

How your funds are divided relies in part on the state in which you live. In most states, your assets are subject to equitable distribution during a divorce settlement. This means that 401(k) assets accumulated during your marriage will be divided, but not necessarily 50-50. Other factors, such as the division of the rest of your marital assets, the length of your marriage, or what each of you has contributed to the marriage will also play a part in the decision. However, if you live in a state with a community property law, you may face an equal split in your 401(k) assets regardless of the other division of marital assets. Following is a list of states that include the community property law:

- Arizona
- California
- Idaho
- Louisiana
- Nevada
- New Mexico
- Texas
- Washington
- Wisconsin

What to Do with QDRO Assets

If you have recently gone through a divorce and will receive money from a QDRO, you have several options. Taking the money in cash can be useful to get through the rough divorce period, but keeping the assets within a tax-sheltered plan would be far more beneficial. If you receive a lump-sum distribution you will have to pay taxes on the entire amount immediately and you will lose the investing and earning power of that money for the future.

Instead, consider leaving the money in your former spouse's 401(k) plan or rolling it over into an IRA. If you would like to leave it in the 401(k) plan, you can make this stipulation part of the QDRO agreement. When the money is divided, the plan's administrator will create a separate account for you. You may not be able to add to this account or withdraw from it until your former spouse withdraws his or her money at retirement, but you will be able to manage the investments of this money yourself and keep it safely tax-sheltered. If you would instead prefer an account that you can make contributions to, rolling the money into an IRA is the best option. Rolling the money into an account not connected with your former spouse also provides you with more freedom as you are allowed to withdraw the money at your own discretion.

401(k) and
Your Rights

20

The people running your plan—including plan trustees, administrators, and investment managers—are known as *fiduciaries.* The law requires these fiduciaries to meet a high standard of conduct in their handling of your money and the administration of your plan. If any of your fiduciaries do not follow the rules, they are personally liable to the plan for all losses suffered as a result. Even in a minor misstep or mistake, this can be costly for them and the company. Also, the largest account balance in the plan probably belongs to the CEO. You can be sure that your CEO is watching carefully over his or her money and, because everyone is treated the same in a 401(k), your money as well. For these reasons, mismanagement of 401(k) plans is rare.

However, 401(k) plans are not entirely free of errors, and some bureaucratic process or paperwork may slip through the cracks. Signs that such a problem may exist include:

- You find errors in your account statements.
- Your account statements are late.
- Contributions are not deposited in a timely manner.
- Your money is not invested as you have allocated.

If these are just minor clerical errors, contacting your human resources department should clear them up. But what if these problems continue to occur? What if your plan is among the tiny percentage of plans where serious wrongdoing is taking place? If this is the case, other warning signs may include:

- Management of your plan keeps changing hands.
- Former employees are having trouble receiving benefits.

If you suspect that your plan is being improperly managed, you need to know your rights in order to take the proper action. Under the Employee Retirement Income Security Act (ERISA) you have the following rights as a 401(k) plan participant:

- The right to receive documentation on plan information
- The right to a timely and fair claims process
- The right to sue for benefits and breaches of fiduciary duty

Plan Documents

By law, your plan must provide in writing the information necessary to understand your 401(k) plan. This information includes plan rules, the financial facts of your plan, and any documents on the operation and management of the plan. Some of this information must be provided regularly and automatically by your plan administrator. Other pieces of information are only available upon request, free of charge, or with copying fees. If you would like to receive these materials, make a request in writing to your human resources department.

The most important document regarding your plan, which you must by law receive, is the summary plan description (SPD). If you have questions about the design of your plan and the way its various features work, consult your SPD. The SPD information includes:

- The name of your plan administrator
- Your plan's eligibility and vesting requirements
- How your contributions and any matching contributions will be deposited
- The details on taking a loan, hardship withdrawal, or distribution

You should receive your SPD when you join your company's 401(k) plan or shortly thereafter. You may also request a copy of your SPD from your human resources department at any time. If the way your plan is designed is changed, you must be informed, either through a revised SPD or in a separate document called a summary of material modifications (SMM), which must also be provided automatically and free of charge.

Filing a Claim

By law, every 401(k) plan must establish a grievance and appeals process for you. The SPD provides two key pieces of information: how your plan's claims process works and an explanation of your legal rights. For example, if you are denied 401(k) benefits to which you feel entitled, you must file a claim.

Filing a claim usually involves filling out specific paperwork and providing certain information about your situation. You may be required to submit evidence to support your claim. If for any reason information on how to file a claim is not provided, you may give notification that you have a claim by writing to your plan administrator, your human resources department, or the department where other kinds of claims at your company are normally filed.

Within 90 days after you have filed a claim, your plan must respond to you. If your claim is denied, the plan administrator must notify you in writing and explain in detail why it was denied. Also, if because of special circumstances your plan needs more time to examine your request, you must be so informed within the 90 days that additional time is needed, why it is needed, and the date by which the plan expects to render a final decision. If you receive no answer at all in 90 days—or 180 days when an extension of time is needed—the claim is considered a denial.

If your claim has been denied, you may appeal the decision. This appeals process, and where to send your appeal, is also listed among the rights and procedures detailed in your SPD. You have at least 60 days (the plan may provide you with more time) in which to file your appeal. If review of your appeal is going to take longer than 60 days, you must be notified in writing of the delay. Except where the review is made by a committee or board of trustees which meets only quarterly, a decision on your appeal must be made within 120 days after you have filed it.

Once the final decision has been made, you must be told the reason and the plan rules upon which the decision was based. This explanation must be written in a manner that you can understand. If you do not receive a notice within the waiting time, you can assume that your claim has been denied after it was reviewed. If your claim is denied and you want to continue to pursue it, you will need to seek legal advice.

Going to the Government

If you believe your employer is not operating your 401(k) plan according to the law, you may contact the government agencies that oversee 401(k) plans. Depending on the illegal activities involved, consider the following government organizations:

- The Department of Labor's Pension and Welfare Benefits Administration can handle improper management of 401(k) assets by a fiduciary, including wrongful investment activities.
- The FBI will assist you when criminal wrongdoing is suspected.

Contact the government agency in writing, keeping your description of the situation short. Provide complete evidence of your accusation, including your plan's SPD and any other relevant plan agreement documentation. If your company will not release information to you or you wish to avoid alerting your company of your process, call the Pension and Welfare Benefits Administration at its Office of Technical Assistance, 202-219-8776, for aid in retrieving information. The government agency you consult with will investigate and, if they find wrongdoing has occurred, attempt to resolve the situation voluntarily. If that fails, they may take action in the form of a lawsuit.

If for some reason you want to contact the government in writing, direct your correspondence to:

U.S. Department of Labor
Pension and Welfare Benefits Administration
Public Disclosure Room, Room N-1513
200 Constitution Avenue, NW
Washington, DC 20210

21

Avoiding 401(k) Mistakes

On your road toward a successful retirement, there are a number of pitfalls that could slow you down. Even the most sophisticated 401(k) participant can make seemingly basic mistakes that could cause problems later on—for example, not maximizing a company match or not rebalancing investment allocation at least every year. Following is a list of the most common errors and some tips on how to avoid them.

Not Participating

You're too busy. You're too young. You don't have the money right now. Let's face it—there will always be some excuse for postponing your 401(k) participation. But saving for retirement in a 401(k) is so important that you should get started now, even if you have 100 reasons not to.

Not saving for retirement early is the number one regret of retirees. Like you, they thought they could start saving in a few years when it became more convenient. But each year they didn't save meant less company match, less compounding, and less at the end of the road. You may think that waiting now will have no effect on an event so far into the future. You're wrong. Waiting has enormous consequences. Remember, you may be fortunate enough to live to be 100, and you will need money on which to survive.

Not Maximizing the Match

The second greatest regret of retirees is that they didn't take full advantage of their employer's match. While you are employed, this is an opportunity for an ongoing boost to your retirement savings. But just like our excuses about not participating, we all have excuses for not contributing the maximum amount to receive the full match. Your reasons, however logical they seem, could prevent you from having enough in retirement.

The very worst excuse is that the company match is too small to be of consequence. In fact, the opposite is true. Even the smallest match is worthwhile because it is free money from your company. Once you retire and must live off of your retirement savings, you will be missing every free penny you could have gained if you had only maximized the match.

Investing Outside Your 401(k) First

Once you have contributed the maximum amount to your 401(k) plan, you should definitely contribute to an IRA, mutual fund, or other outside investment account. The more you have for retirement, the better. But don't contribute anywhere else until you have maxed out your 401(k) plan. In no other type of investment program will you receive the special 401(k) design features, along with pretax saving and compounding.

Not Investing for the Long Term

When you have a long-term time horizon for your investments you should follow your asset allocation plan come what may. This means avoiding emotional decisions based on the performance of the market. If you invest too much of your assets in safe funds that provide a low rate of return, you will not build enough money for retirement. If your investments are speculative in the hopes of dramatic growth, you risk taking a hit if you need your money during a time when the stock market is falling.

The goal of 401(k) plan investing is average investment returns that remain steady over time. If you focus on the short-term fluctuations of the market you will never use that long-term time horizon to its best advantage. Patient investors who are willing to wait will reap the rewards of compounding and planning when they retire.

Overtrading

When some people purchase stocks through a 401(k) plan, they begin to think they can be day traders. They start by purchasing last year's best stocks or expert favorites in the hopes that these shooting stars will continue to skyrocket. Then they try to time the market, following the market prices every day so they can buy or sell at just the right time. Unfortunately, before too long a market correction drops the price of one of their sure wins, teaching them about long-term investing the hard way.

Sound familiar? When you buy and sell stocks too often it is called overtrading. This practice not only puts your retirement assets at risk if the market falls, it also eats away at your principal through fees. Frequent buying and selling generates administrative costs. If you are overtrading, those fees can take a real toll on the 401(k) account you have worked so hard to build.

Not Rebalancing

When you created your asset allocation plan, you decided that a certain mix of investment choices was right for you—for example, 60 percent stocks and 40 percent bonds. But short-term changes can result in a different distribution of your assets from year to year. Your original asset allocation can easily shift if one side of your investments does better than the other or one side rises while the other falls. In fact, your allocation percentages can move far off the mark—for example, 80 percent in stocks and 20 percent in bonds. If you do not periodically rebalance these assets, moving money around so that the percentage returns to your original allocation, you risk having the market make the change for you—when the market drops. Besides, rebalancing forces you to sell high and buy low, increasing your overall investment return.

Misunderstanding Bond Funds

Confusing a 401(k) bond fund with a bond is a common mistake that can cause you very real problems. When you create your asset allocation, part of your money will always be invested in more conservative funds to balance out your more aggressive choices. Bonds are a fairly secure investment because they return your original investment to you, plus any earnings, on the date of the bond's maturity. Many think that bond funds carry the same security and invest the conservative portion of their asset allocation in this investment choice, not knowing that the value of bond funds can fluctuate.

Unlike a bond, a bond fund never matures. This means that you may not get back the amount of your original investment, called your principal, if changes in interest rates reduce the value of bonds in your bond fund. Bond funds have the potential to earn a much greater rate of return than bonds, but they also carry a much greater potential to lose money—the definition of a more aggressive investment option. Do not invest in a bond fund if you want an investment that will not decline in value.

Borrowing for Nonemergencies

Having access to your 401(k) assets in case of emergency is one of the great advantages of 401(k) plans. When you suddenly need your money, you may be able to call an 800 number and have the cash in your hands in a matter of days. You can feel free to contribute the maximum amount to your 401(k) plan because you know those funds will never be out of reach.

But that easy access can be a little too easy for some. Is a big vacation really an emergency? If your 401(k) money were not available, you could easily find ways to cover these expenses—or do without. That is exactly how you should address every urge to take a 401(k) loan, even for more reasonable costs such as the purchase of a primary home or paying for your child's college education. Withdrawing from your account may alter your asset allocation, seriously reduce your compounding, and decrease the amount you will have at retirement. Then, if you end employment while you have an outstanding loan, you may be forced to repay the outstanding amount immediately.

Cashing Out before Retirement

When you change jobs it may be tempting to take your money out of your 401(k) plan as a distribution. Don't do it. You will face a 10 percent early withdrawal federal income tax penalty and 20 percent income tax withholding, as well as eventually having to pay full regular state and federal income taxes. Having some cash in your pocket is not worth the sizeable chunk the government will take out. More importantly, you are depriving yourself of plan assets that are critical for building a successful retirement.

Instead, when you change jobs you can roll that money over to your new employer's plan, keep it in your old employer's plan, or transfer the money to an IRA. This keeps the assets tax-sheltered and allows the compounding growth of your money to continue.

Conclusion
401(k)—The Plan That Pays

From bustles to bellbottoms, many things once fashionable are now out of style. Sooner or later, every idea and product is updated, revised, and improved. It's called progress, and savings plans are no exception. Just as a covered wagon is an old-fashioned vehicle compared to a car, a regular savings plan is an old-fashioned retirement savings vehicle compared to a 401(k) plan.

When Section 401(k) of the Internal Revenue Code created this savings opportunity, it took a good idea—saving for the future—and made it even better. Your 401(k) plan is a better way to save because:

- It's easy to use.
- It provides immediate and ongoing tax advantages.
- It helps you get more mileage from your money.

Saving in a 401(k) is more convenient and more effective than an ordinary savings account, and it actually pays you money when you save. That's good news, because saving for the future won't fall out of fashion.

To maintain the lifestyle you've come to expect, you will need substantial personal savings when you retire. But it's not always easy to think about saving for the future. Before your paycheck even reaches you it starts to shrink. Taxes take a big bite, and what's left can disappear before you know it. The trick to saving for the future is to pay yourself first.

This is where your company's 401(k) plan comes in. To help you save for the future, your company has provided you with an easier and faster way to make your money grow. How? Your 401(k) plan puts your future security first. Each pay period your 401(k) contribution is automatically deducted from your paycheck and placed in your 401(k) plan, allowing you to enjoy substantial tax advantages. Because your 401(k) contribution takes place before taxes, it is exempt from federal taxes and you can save more money than in a regular account.

In addition, you're in the driver's seat when you save through 401(k) because you decide how much to put into the plan. Although government regulations limit 401(k) contributions, they allow you to put more money into a 401(k) plan than into an IRA. 401(k) can carry you closer to financial security in retirement. Doesn't it make sense to put your money where it will go the farthest?

If you remember to follow these eight principles from Chapter 9 and take care of your 401(k) plan, your 401(k) plan will take care of you.

1. Start with an investment plan.
2. Invest for long-term gain.
3. Diversify your investments.
4. Use reasonable assumptions.
5. Stay with your plan.
6. Rebalance at least annually.
7. Keep your money invested for as long as possible.
8. Understand the emotions of investing.

In addition to the tips listed in Chapter 9, which will apply throughout your 401(k) career, be sure to transition your investments as you approach retirement, as we discuss in Chapter 14.

Like superconducters, DVDs, and the Internet, 401(k) plans are the future. This book has given you all the tools you need to make the most of your 401(k). Congratulations. With your new knowledge and expertise, you're ready to take control of your financial future with your 401(k) plan!

Frequently Asked Questions

A

Courtesy of the Profit Sharing/401(k) Council of America Web site <www.psca.org>.

How Much Money Can I Put into My 401(k) Account?

Most plans allow you to contribute a percentage of your pay, generally between 1 and 15 percent. The *maximum* pretax contribution dollar amount is set by law and adjusted for inflation annually. The 2002 pretax contribution limit is $11,000, which will increase by $1,000 every year until reaching $15,000 in 2006. After that, the maximum will be indexed to inflation. Some plans may offer you the option to contribute on an after-tax basis, which is not included in the limit. In addition, there are special nondiscrimination rules to prevent the top employees in your company—called highly compensated employees (HCE)—from being able to save substantially more than lower-paid employees.

What Is the Difference between Investing Pretax and After-Tax Contributions?

The difference between the two types of contributions is when you are taxed. Pretax contributions and earnings are taxed only when you withdraw the money from your plan. Because the money that would normally be paid in taxes goes directly into the plan, pretax contributions can accumulate quickly. However, if you need to withdraw money prior to age 59¹/₂, you may incur a 10 percent early withdrawal federal income tax penalty, in addition to owing current regular income taxes. After-tax contributions are taxed before they are put into the plan. Although you won't owe taxes on your contributions when you take a withdrawal, you will be taxed on the earnings and may be subject to an early withdrawal penalty on the interest earned if you do so before age 59½.

What Pretax Percentage Should I Invest When I Am Starting Out?

Don't delay participating and contributing to your plan because you are just starting out, you don't make much money, or you can't contribute much now for financial reasons. Any savings is better than nothing and the sooner you get started, the better! Also, be sure to take full advantage of your company's match. For example, if your company matches 50 cents on the dollar up to 6 percent, you should contribute at least 6 percent. Simply defer as much as you can afford to budget and maximize the tax deferral.

Is It Legal for My Employer to Move My 401(k) Account Balances to Similar Investment Funds and Change Investment Fund Managers?

It is legal, but it is your company's responsibility to provide a diverse selection of competitively performing funds.

What Can I Do If I Don't Like the Investment Funds That My Company Offers?

Talk to your human resources representative. Your employer has implemented a retirement savings plan for your use and your benefit and they want to know if you are dissatisfied with your plan.

Can I Withdraw Money from My Account While I Am Still Working?

Some plans offer loans allowing you to borrow money from your 401(k) account. However, this money comes out of one of your investments so you will not receive the investment return you expected. Instead, you will be paying interest to the plan. If you fail to pay back the loan, it is treated as a withdrawal and the outstanding loan balance will be subject to current income taxes as well as a 10 percent early withdrawal federal income tax penalty. If you leave your job for any reason, you will be required to pay back your loan.

Some other common features of loans include:

- Plans typically allow you to borrow 50 percent of your plan assets, up to $50,000, less any outstanding loan balances.
- The interest rate you pay will be determined on the day you take the loan, and will be fixed for a five-year repayment period.
- In cases where the loan is a mortgage for your primary residence, the payment period may be longer.
- While interest rates vary by plan, a loan made from a 401(k) plan usually has an interest rate of prime plus 1 percent.

If your plan doesn't offer loans, you may be able to qualify for a hardship withdrawal if no other resources are available to you.

What Are the Rules Regarding Hardship Withdrawals from My 401(k)?

Hardship withdrawals are allowed by law but your employer is not required to provide this option in your plan. The cost of administering such a program can be prohibitive for many small companies. Your summary plan description (SPD) will state whether or not your employer allows withdrawals in your plan. The IRS code that governs 401(k) plans provides for hardship withdrawals only if you meet the following five conditions:

1. The withdrawal is due to an immediate and heavy financial need.
2. The withdrawal is necessary to satisfy that need (i.e., you have no other funds or way to meet the need).
3. The withdrawal does not exceed the amount you need (plus the amount you need to pay taxes on the withdrawal).
4. You have first obtained all distribution or nontaxable loans available under the 401k plan.
5. You don't contribute to the 401(k) plan for 6 months (previously 12 months) following the withdrawal.

The following three items are considered by the IRS as acceptable reasons for a hardship withdrawal:

1. Down payment for purchase of primary residence.
2. College expenses for you or your dependents.

3. Medical expenses that exceed 7.5 percent of your adjusted gross income.

Some companies are more lenient than others. Because of the complexity surrounding this issue and varying plan designs, you need to reference your plan document or ask your human resources representative for further information regarding plan withdrawals.

Hardship withdrawals are subject to income tax and, if you are not at least 59½ years of age, a 10 percent early withdrawal federal income tax penalty as well. You are not allowed to pay the withdrawal amount back.

How Does a Company Match Work?

A company can choose from among several different 401(k) matching approaches, the most common being a fixed match. A fixed match is based on a set percentage of the employee contribution. The most common fixed matching approach is an employer contribution of 50 cents for every dollar that the employee contributes, up to an employee contribution of 6 percent of pay.

Some companies have a graded match. This means that the percentage contributed by the company will vary depending upon the percentage of pay contributed by the participant. The most common graded match is a company contribution equal to 100 percent of the first 3 percent of pay contributed by the employee, and 50 percent of the next 2 percent of pay that the participant contributes.

A few companies base their 401(k) matching contribution on your years of service with the company. One company with this type of matching program matches up to 8 percent of pay based on the following schedule of service:

- 25 percent for those with one to five years of service
- 50 percent for those with six to ten years of service
- 75 percent for those with 11 to 15 years of service
- 100 percent for those with more than 15 years of service

As you can see, companies have wide latitude in how they design their matching program. The matching formula for your plan will be outlined in detail in your SPD.

Can I Stop Contributing If I Feel I Can't Afford It?

Most plans allow you to stop contributing at any time, though employers are not required *by law* to do so. Some plans may require a minimum contribution for a full plan year, so be sure to check your plan rules. Also be aware that if you suspend all contributions you may be prohibited from contributing again for a period of time.

What Happens to My 401(k) Account Balances If I Choose to Leave or I Am Fired from the Company?

Your distribution options are the same whether you voluntarily leave or are terminated. If your account balance is more than $5,000, you can leave your money in the plan. If you want to take your money with you, your vested account balance can be rolled into another 401(k) plan with your employer or put into an IRA to avoid early withdrawal penalties.

How Long Can My Former Company Hold My Account Balance from My Date of Termination?

There is no quick, general answer. There are four factors that affect the timing of your distribution:

1. *Your plan.* The plan itself may provide a time frame, which can be found in your plan documentation or summary plan description. In some rare cases, distributions are not made until the participant has reached retirement age, usually defined as age 65, even if you terminated employment much earlier.
2. *Your next valuation date.* Your distribution cannot be processed until after the next valuation date, when the plan determines the account balances of participants. Companies can determine account balances daily, monthly, quarterly, semiannually, or even annually.
3. *Your investments.* How your money is invested can affect how long it will take for you to get your distribution. While most investments can be liquidated quickly, a few—such as some real estate investments—may take longer.

4. *Your paperwork.* Processing your paperwork after the valuation date can take a few days or a few weeks depending on how your plan is managed. It is important for you to know that your company wants you to have your money just as soon as you do. The company is responsible for and must pay fees on your account balance for as long as your money remains in the plan.

What Information and Reports Is My Employer Required to Provide to Me Regarding My 401(k) Plan?

Your employer must provide you with a summary plan description, which provides all the general information about your plan, and an annual statement that details your personal account information. In addition, you will often be provided a prospectus for every fund offered in the plan, but this is not legally required. If your company's stock is offered in the plan, you likely will receive a prospectus on the company stock fund, although some companies make this part of the SPD. You have a legal right to ask the plan administrator for a copy of the following: the summary plan description, the plan document, the trust agreement for funding the plan (if separate from the plan), the plan's latest Form 5500 or Form 5500-C/R, any collective bargaining contract, if appropriate, and any other document under which the plan was established or is operated.

How Soon Does My Employer Have to Deposit My Contributions Deducted from My Pay into My 401(k) Account?

By law, your contributions to a 401(k) must be deposited to the plan on the earliest date that they can be reasonably segregated from the employer's general assets. The date of deposit may not be later than the fifteenth business day of the month following the month in which your contributions are deducted from your pay. Please note: Your employer cannot wait until the fifteenth business day of the month following the month in which your contribution was deducted just for the convenience of doing so. If your employer can deposit the funds sooner, it must do so.

I Still Have a 401(k) Account with My Former Employer. I Would Like to Transfer This Account into My IRA. Can This Be Done? If So, Are There Any Penalties?

Yes, this can be done. It is referred to as a trustee-to-trustee transfer. You need to request the distribution forms from your former employer. Make sure you open your new IRA before the transfer so that you can provide the account information on the required forms (this may require a minimum opening balance). There are no penalties and no withholding with a trustee-to-trustee transfer. However, if you allow your former employer to send the funds directly to you (rather than to your new IRA), your employer will be required to deduct and remit 20 percent of the total to the IRS.

I Am Currently Working in the United States on a Visa. If I Choose to Leave the United States When My Visa Expires, What Will Happen with My 401(k) Account?

There are no special provisions for those working in the United States on a visa. To avoid early withdrawal penalties and payment of taxes you can do one of three things:

1. If your account balance is over $5,000, you can leave your 401(k) money in your former employer's plan.
2. You can roll your account balance into an IRA.
3. You can request a distribution from the 401(k) plan and take the lump-sum payment. If you decide to take your distribution in cash you will have to pay regular income taxes and the 10 percent early withdrawal federal income tax penalty when you take the lump-sum payment.

B

401(k)
A Brief History

Courtesy of the Profit Sharing/401(k) Council of America Web site <www.psca.org>.

In 1974, Congress enacted the Employee Retirement Income Security Act (ERISA), the first comprehensive pension reform law. ERISA was a massive and complex piece of legislation, and plan sponsors had difficulty understanding how to comply. For example, it was unclear whether qualified cash or deferred arrangements (CODA plans) were still permitted.

After the passage of ERISA, groups in support of deferred profit sharing programs urged Congress to enact legislation clarifying that the CODA practice continue to be permitted. This led to the passage of Section 401(k) to the Internal Revenue Code in 1978. The number of employers and employees benefiting from Section 401(k) was initially minimal as employers waited for regulatory clarification of the law. Then in 1981, the Internal Revenue Service (IRS) published its regulations clarifying Section 401(k). These regulations allowed employees to contribute regular earnings as well as profit sharing bonuses on an income tax-deferred and a Federal Insurance Contribution Act (FICA) tax-exempt basis. Companies quickly added the new tax-deferred contribution arrangement to their existing thrift-savings and deferred profit sharing programs, and plan growth exploded.

Section 401(k), designed to reinstate and add to the CODA plan, has instead replaced most CODA plans. The 401(k) plan combines the advantageous cash and deferred aspects of the CODA plan with unique features like pretax salary reduction, making it an extremely sought-after retirement investment choice.

Contribution Limits through 2010

Courtesy of the Profit Sharing/401(k) Council of America Web site <www.psca.org>.

Following are the contribution limits for 401(k) plans, 403(b) plans, 457 plans, SEP plans, SIMPLE plans, and IRAs. Also included are the limits for catch-up contributions under these plans. More information on catch-up contributions and other new regulations under EGTRRA can be found in Appendix D. Contribution limits are accurate through December 31, 2010.

	2002	2003	2004	2005	2006	2007	2008	2009	2010
401(k), 403(b), and SEP contribution limits	$11,000	$12,000	$13,000	$14,000	$15,000	Indexed in $500 increments			
SIMPLE IRAs and SIMPLE 401(k) limits	$7,000	$8,000	$9,000	$10,000		Indexed in $500 increments			
457 contribution limits	$11,000	$12,000	$13,000	$14,000	$15,000	Indexed in $500 increments			
401(k), 403(b), and SEP catch-up contributions	$1,000	$2,000	$3,000	$4,000	$5,000	Indexed in $500 increments			
SIMPLE IRA and SIMPLE 401(k) catch-up contributions	$500	$1,000	$1,500	$2,000	$2,500	Indexed in $500 increments			
IRA contribution limits	$3,000	$3,000	$3,000	$4,000	$4,000	$4,000	$5,000	Indexed in $500 increments	
IRA catch-up contributions	$500	$500	$500	$500	$1,000				

The Economic Growth and Tax Relief Reconciliation Act of 2001 Provisions Affecting Your 401(k) Plan

Courtesy of the Profit Sharing/401(k) Council of America Web site <www.psca.org>.

On May 26, 2001, Congress passed the Economic Growth and Tax Relief Reconciliation Act of 2001 (EGTRRA), and on June 7, 2001, President Bush signed the act into law. This legislation contains a number of provisions relating to 401(k) plans. The two main purposes of these EGTRRA provisions were to increase retirement savings, especially for employees of small employers, and to reduce administrative burdens on plan sponsors. In particular, EGTRRA:

- Increased annual limitations and elective contribution limitations (including higher contribution limits for older workers) for 401(k) plans and individual retirement accounts (IRAs).
- Increased portability of 401(k) plan benefits, including transfers of benefits in merger and acquisition transactions.
- Eased administrative complexities for 401(k) plans.

EGTRRA provisions are scheduled to "sunset" (end) for plan years beginning on or after January 1, 2011. This means that unless future lawmakers decide to extend some or all of the EGTRRA provisions, beginning in 2011, 401(k) plans and IRAs will need to comply with pre-EGTRRA law.

The following summary highlights some of the major EGTRRA provisions that might affect your 401(k) plan. Unless otherwise noted, the effective date for the provisions discussed in the summary is plan years beginning on or after January 1, 2002.

Increased Contribution and Benefit Limitations

Before EGTRRA, the maximum annual contributions that could be made on behalf of participants to 401(k) plans was 25 percent of compensation or $35,000 (whichever was less). This amount was indexed for cost-of-living adjustments in $5,000 increments. EGTRRA provided the following changes to the maximum annual contributions:

- Increased the annual limit on employer and employee contributions to $40,000.
- Allowed faster cost-of-living adjustments ($1,000 increments instead of $5,000 increments).
- Increased the 25 percent of compensation limit to 100 percent of compensation.

Compensation Limitations

Before EGTRRA, $170,000 was the maximum amount of a participant's compensation that could be taken into account for plan purposes. This amount was indexed for cost-of-living adjustments in $10,000 increments. EGTRRA has increased the maximum compensation amount to $200,000, which is now indexed for cost-of-living adjustments in $5,000 increments.

Contribution Limitations

Before EGTRRA, $10,500 was the maximum dollar amount of employee-deferred contributions that could be made to a 401(k) plan, a tax-deferred annuity arrangement of a tax-exempt employer (a 403(b) plan), or a simplified employee pension plan (SEP). This amount was indexed for cost-of-living adjustments in $500 increments. EGTRRA has increased this dollar limit to

- $11,000 for the year 2002, and

- an additional $1,000 for each subsequent year beginning in 2003 until the limit reaches $15,000 in 2006.

Thereafter, the present law's cost-of-living adjustment would apply ($500 increments). EGTRRA has also increased the maximum elective deferral limit for SIMPLE plans (i.e., special tax-favored plans for small employers) and deferred compensation plans of state or local governments or tax-exempt organizations (457 plans). For 457 plans, EGTRRA also repeals the rules coordinating the dollar limit under such plans with contributions made under 401(k) and 403(b) plans.

Expansion of Deduction Limits on Employer Contributions

Before EGTRRA, an employer sponsoring a defined contribution plan (including a 401(k) plan) could deduct only contributions made to such a plan that did not exceed 15 percent of the covered compensation of employees eligible to participate in the plan. In the case of a 401(k) plan, salary deferral contributions by employees were considered employer contributions and counted towards the 15 percent limit. EGTRRA increased the maximum employer deduction applicable to defined contribution plan employer contributions to 25 percent of the total covered compensation of plan participants. In addition, employee salary deferral contributions no longer count toward the limit.

Roth 401(k) Contribution Accounts

Beginning in 2006, EGTRRA permits Roth contributions to 401(k) or 403(b) plans. Under EGTRRA, Roth contributions are not tax deductible, but there is no tax on distributions of such amounts, including earnings. To the extent that a plan permits Roth contributions, the plan administrator would be required to establish a separate account and maintain separate record keeping for such nondeductible contributions.

Tax Credit for Elective Deferrals and IRA Contributions

EGTRRA provides for a temporary tax credit for certain employee contributions made to a 401(k) plan. The maximum annual contribution eligible for the credit is $2,000 and the amount of the credit depends on the participant's adjusted gross income (AGI). The credit is available to

- a single taxpayer with AGI of $25,000 or less,
- a taxpayer filing as head of household with AGI of $37,500 or less, or
- taxpayers filing jointly with AGI of $50,000 or less.

This credit is generally available for years 2002 through 2006 to individuals who are between 18 and 60 years old.

Catch-Up Contributions

EGTRRA increased the dollar limits on employee salary deferral contributions under 401(k) plans for those reaching age 50 by the end of the applicable plan year. The additional amount of elective contributions that may be made by an eligible individual participating in such a plan is $1,000 for 2002, $2,000 in 2003, $3,000 in 2004, $4,000 in 2005, and $5,000 in 2006. After 2006, the amount is indexed to cost-of-living adjustments in $500 increments. For SIMPLE plans, all amounts referenced are one half of the amount above. The additional contributions are not subject to any other limits, including plan-imposed percentage limits or nondiscrimination testing requirements.

Faster Vesting of Employer Matching Contributions

Before EGTRRA, five-year cliff or seven-year graded were the maximum permissible vesting schedules. Under five-year cliff vesting, a participant was 100 percent vested after completing five years of service (and 0 percent vested before that time). Under seven-year graded vesting, a participant owned 20 percent of the matching contribution for each year of service (beginning with the participant's third year of service), so that the participant was 100 percent vested after seven years.

EGTRRA requires accelerated vesting schedules for employer matching contributions (but not other employer contributions, including profit sharing) to 401(k) plans. Now, *three-year cliff* or *six-year graded* are the maximum permissible vesting schedules. Under three-year cliff vesting, a participant is 100 percent vested after completing three years of service (and 0 percent vested before such time). Under six-year graded vesting, a participant owns 20 percent of the employer matching contributions for each year of service (beginning with the participant's second year of service), so that the participant is 100 percent vested after six years of service. The accelerated vesting schedules will apply to contributions for plan years beginning in 2002. Employer matching contributions subject to a collective bargaining agreement will have a delayed effective date until 2006.

Hardship Withdrawals

The U.S. Department of Treasury regulations provide a safe harbor under which a 401(k) plan distribution may be treated as a hardship withdrawal. Generally, a hardship withdrawal may only be taken to satisfy the following immediate and heavy financial needs:

- Medical expenses
- Educational expenses
- Expenses relating to the purchase of a primary residence

Before EGTRRA, taking a hardship withdrawal under the safe harbor prohibited an employee from making salary deferral contributions to the plan for at least 12 months after receiving the hardship withdrawal. EGTRRA shortened the 12-month suspension to a six-month suspension period and made other related changes.

Expanded Rollover Options

Pre-EGTRRA law regarding rollovers stated the following:

- An eligible rollover distribution from a 401(k) plan may be rolled over on a tax-free basis to a traditional IRA or another 401(k) plan.
- Eligible rollover distributions from a 403(b) plan may be rolled over into a traditional IRA or another 403(b) plan.
- Distributions (other than required minimum distributions) from a traditional IRA can be rolled over into another traditional IRA.
- Distributions from a 457 plan can only be transferred to another 457 plan.
- After-tax employee contributions cannot be rolled over.
- A surviving spouse that receives an eligible rollover distribution may only roll over the distribution into an IRA, not a 401(k) plan.

EGTRRA expanded the available rollover options. Rollover distributions from 401(k) plans, 403(b) plans, and 457 plans are now permitted to 401(k) plans, 403(b) plans, or 457 plans. IRA distributions may be rolled over to 401(k) plans, 403(b) plans, and 457 plans. In addition, employee after-tax contributions may be rolled over into a traditional IRA or another 401(k) plan (provided the recipient plan provides for separate accounting for such funds and associated earnings). However, in the case of a rollover from one 401(k) plan to another, an after-tax contribution may only be transferred through direct trustee-to-trustee transfers. After-tax contributions still cannot be rolled over from an IRA into a 401(k) plan, 403(b) plan, or 457 plan. EGTRRA also allows a surviving spouse to make a rollover distribution into a 401(k) plan, 403(b) plan, or 457 plan in which such spouse participates.

Waiver of 60-Day Rule

Before EGTRRA, money received from a 401(k) plan or IRA could be rolled over tax-free if the rollover was made within 60 days of the date of distribution. EGTRRA allows the Secretary of the Treasury to waive the 60-day rollover period if the failure to waive such requirement would be "against equity or good conscience." This could be allowed when the failure to roll over within 60 days was caused by casualty, disaster, or other events beyond the reasonable control of the individual attempting the rollover.

Disregarding Rollovers in Applying the Cash-Out Rules

When a 401(k) plan participant terminates employment, present law allows the plan to cash-out the employee's account (i.e., distribute without the recipient's consent) as long as the account value is less than $5,000. EGTRRA allows a plan to disregard any amount that was rolled into the plan for purposes of determining the present value of a participant's account. This means that accounts in excess of $5,000 may, to the extent that the nonrollover portion of such account does not exceed $5,000, be distributed.

ESOP Dividends May Be Reinvested without Loss of Dividend Deduction

Present law entitles an employer to deduct certain dividends paid in cash during the employer's taxable year for company stock held by an employee stock ownership plan (ESOP). This deduction is allowed for dividends that are

- paid in cash directly to the plan participants or their beneficiaries,
- paid to the plan and subsequently distributed to the participants or their beneficiaries in cash no later than 90 days after the close of the plan year in which the dividends are paid to the plan, or
- used to make payments on loans that were used to acquire the employer securities with respect to which the dividend is paid.

EGTRRA allows an employer to make additional deductions for dividends that, at the request of plan participants or their beneficiaries, are *payable* (though not paid) with respect to the first two points above, or are paid to the plan and then reinvested in qualifying employer securities. The Secretary of the Treasury may disallow the deduction if it is determined that the dividend constitutes an avoidance or evasion of tax, or if the amount of the dividend is unreasonable.

Employer-Provided Retirement Advice

Present law excludes certain employer-provided fringe benefits from gross income and wages for employment tax purposes. These excludable fringe benefits include working condition fringe benefits and *de minimis* fringes, as well as certain employer-provided educational assistance. EGTRRA provides that the value of certain retirement planning services provided to an employee and his or her spouse by an employer maintaining a 401(k) plan are also excludable from income and wages. The exclusion does not apply with respect to highly compensated employees unless the services are available on substantially the same terms to each member of the group of employees normally provided such education and information (for example, only those employees nearing retirement age).

Automatic Rollovers of Certain Cash-Out Distributions

Before EGTRRA, if a participant terminated employment, a 401(k) plan could distribute the participant's account to the participant without his or her consent, as long as the value of the account did not exceed $5,000. EGTRRA provides that direct rollovers must be the default option for cash-out distributions that exceed $1,000, which are eligible rollover distributions from 401(k) plans. Such distribution is required to be rolled over automatically to a designated IRA, unless the participant affirmatively elects to have the distribution transferred to a different IRA or another 401(k) plan, or to receive the account balance directly.

EGTRRA requires the plan administrator to provide a written notice explaining that an automatic direct rollover will be made unless the participant elects otherwise, and that the distribution may be later transferred by the participant without cost to another IRA. This provision is not effective until the Department of Labor issues rules explaining its implementation, but no later than 2004.

Increased Annual Contribution Limitations to IRAs

There are two types of retirement-oriented IRAs: the traditional IRA and the newer Roth IRA. Before EGTRRA, an individual could make tax-deductible contributions up to $2,000 to one IRA per year. EGTRRA increased the maximum annual dollar contribution limit applicable to both traditional and Roth IRAs from $2,000 to $3,000 for the years 2002 through 2004; $4,000 for the years 2005 through 2007; and $5,000 for the year 2008. Thereafter, the limit will be adjusted annually for inflation in increments of $500.

In addition, EGTRRA allows individuals who have turned 50 years old during a taxable year to make *extra* catch-up contributions. The otherwise applicable limit for such individuals is increased by $500 for the years 2002 through 2005, and $1,000 for the year 2006 and thereafter.

Based on material provided by Kenneth A. Raskin and Richard C. Libert of White & Case, LLP, New York City, New York.

Glossary of Terms

English

401(k) plan A defined-contribution plan that permits employees to deduct a portion of their salary from their paycheck and contribute to an account before taxation. Employers may also make contributions to a participant's account, called a company match. Federal (and sometimes state) taxes on contributions and investment earnings are deferred (i.e., postponed) until the participant takes money out of the plan in a distribution (typically at retirement).

403(b) plan Also known as a *tax-sheltered annuity* (TSA), a 403(b) provides a tax shelter for 501(c)(3) tax-exempt employers (which include public schools). Employers qualifying for a 403(b) plan may defer taxes on contributions to certain annuity contracts or custodial accounts.

accrued benefits Retirement benefits earned to date by an employee, which will be expressed in a 401(k) plan in terms of the amount in the employee's account.

actual deferral percentage (ADP) An antidiscrimination test that compares the amount deferred by highly compensated employees to the deferrals of non–highly compensated employees.

asset allocation An employee's division of money between different types of investment choices. An example of asset allocation would be 70 percent stocks and 30 percent bonds.

alternate payee A person other than a plan participant (such as a spouse, former spouse, child, etc.) who, under a domestic relations order (see *qualified domestic relations order*), has a right to receive all or some of a participant's pension benefits.

annual audit Federal law requires that all plans with more than 100 participants be audited by an independent auditor. It is also common to refer to a Department of Labor or IRS examination of a plan as a plan audit.

annual report A document filed annually (Form 5500) with the IRS that reports pension plan information for a particular year, including such items as participation, funding, and administration.

annuity A contract providing retirement income at regular intervals. See also *qualified joint and survivor annuity.*

automatic deferral default percentage The percentage of pay that is taken pretax and put into a plan when an employee is enrolled via an automatic enrollment feature. The typical automatic deferral default percentage is 3 percent of pay. Participants can generally choose to defer an amount other than the default percentage.

automatic enrollment The practice of enrolling all eligible employees in a plan and beginning participant deferrals without requiring the employees to submit a request to participate. Plan design specifies how these automatic deferrals will be invested. Employees who do not want to make contributions must actively file a request to be excluded from the plan. Participants can generally change the amount of pay that is deferred and how it is invested.

beneficiary A person, persons, or trust designated to receive the plan benefits of a participant in the event of the participant's death.

blackout period Also called a lockdown, transitional period or quiet period. This refers to the time when plan participants cannot access their accounts. These periods can be caused by a number of events, including a change in plan record keepers, a change in plan trustees, a change to daily valuation from monthly valuation, or a company merger or acquisition.

cafeteria plan In this plan, employees may chose from a "menu" of two or more benefits.

cash-out The distribution of assets from a plan to a participant prior to retirement, typically occurring when a participant has a balance under $5,000 and leaves a company without requesting to have his or her assets rolled over into an IRA or into a new employer's plan. Cash-outs are subject to federal withholding tax and are subject to the 10 percent early withdrawal federal income tax penalty if taken before age 59½.

cash or deferred arrangement (CODA) A type of profit sharing or stock bonus plan in which employees may defer current pretax compensation.

cash or deferred election A participant request to defer compensation, on a pretax basis, to a CODA plan.

cash profit sharing plan A type of profit sharing plan in which the company makes contributions directly to employees in cash or stock. (This type of profit sharing plan is not a qualified retirement plan.)

cliff vesting A vesting schedule that gives an employee 100 percent ownership of company contributions after a specified number of years of service. (See also *vesting*.)

common control Businesses are under common control when one entity owns at least 80 percent of the stock, profit, or capital interest in the other organization, or when the same five or fewer people own a controlling interest in each entity.

conversion The process of changing from one service provider to another.

deferred profit sharing plan A type of qualified retirement plan in which the company makes contributions to individual participant accounts.

deferral A pretax contribution set aside from an employee's paycheck.

defined-benefit plan A retirement plan in which the sponsoring company provides a certain guaranteed benefit to participants based on a predetermined formula.

defined-contribution plan An employer-sponsored plan in which contributions are made to individual participant accounts, and the final benefit consists solely of assets (including investment returns) that have accumulated in these individual accounts. Depending on the type of defined-contribution plan, contributions may be made either by the company, the participant, or both.

Department of Labor (DOL) The U.S. Department of Labor (DOL) deals with issues related to the American work force—including topics concerning pension and benefit plans. Through its branch agency the Pension and Welfare Benefits Administration, the DOL is responsible for administering the provisions of Title I of ERISA, which regulates proper administration of plans.

disclosure Plan sponsors must provide access to certain types of information for participants, including summary plan descriptions, summary of material modifications, and summary annual reports.

determination letter Document issued by the IRS formally recognizing that the plan meets the qualifications for tax-advantaged treatment.

discrimination testing Tax-qualified retirement plans must be administered in compliance with several regulations requiring numerical measurements. Typically, the process of determining whether the plan is in compliance is collectively called discrimination testing.

distribution Any payout made from a retirement plan. See also lump-sum distribution and annuity.

early withdrawal penalty There is a 10 percent early withdrawal federal income tax penalty for withdrawal of assets from a qualified retirement plan prior to age $59\frac{1}{2}$. This 10 percent early withdrawal federal income tax penalty is in addition to regular federal and state tax (if applicable).

eligibility Conditions that must be met in order to participate in a plan, such as age or length of service requirements.

eligible employees Employees who meet the requirements for participation in an employer-sponsored plan.

employee stock ownership plan (ESOP) A qualified, defined-contribution plan in which plan assets are invested primarily or exclusively in the securities of the sponsoring employer.

ERISA Plan sponsors are required by law to design and administer their plans in accordance with the Employee Retirement Income Security Act of 1974 (ERISA). Among its statutes, ERISA calls for proper plan reporting and disclosure to participants.

ERISA rights statement ERISA requires that this document, explaining participant and beneficiary rights, be included within a summary plan description (SPD).

excess accumulations The amount that a participant's required minimum distribution (after age $70^1/_2$) surpasses the amount distributed. When distributions reach 50 percent above the minimum, they may be taxed.

excess aggregate contributions After-tax participant contributions or matching employer contributions that cause a plan to fail the 401(m) actual contribution percentage (ACP) nondiscrimination test.

excess contributions Pretax participant contributions that cause a plan to fail the 401(k) actual deferral percentage (ADP) nondiscrimination test.

excess benefit plan A plan, or part of a plan, maintained to provide benefits that exceed IRS Code 415 limits on contributions and benefits.

excludable employees The employees that may be excluded from the group being tested during 401(k) nondiscrimination testing. The following are excludable employees, certain ex-employees; certain airline pilots, nonresident aliens with no U.S. source of income, employees who do not meet minimum age and length of service requirements, and employees whose retirement benefits are covered by collective bargaining agreements.

exclusive benefit rule A rule under **ERISA** that says the assets in an employee account may be used for the exclusive benefit of the employee and his or her beneficiaries.

expense ratio The percentage of a fund's assets that are used to pay its annual expenses.

facts and circumstances test The test determining whether financial need exists for a 401(k) hardship withdrawal.

FICA The federal law that taxes employee wages for Social Security and other programs.

fidelity bond Protects participants in the event a fiduciary or other responsible person steals or mishandles plan assets.

fiduciary A person with the authority to make decisions regarding a plan's assets or important administrative matters. Fiduciaries are required under ERISA to make decisions based solely on the best interests of plan participants.

fiduciary insurance Insurance that protects plan fiduciaries in the event that they are found liable for a breach of fiduciary responsibility.

forfeiture Plan assets surrendered by participants upon termination of employment before being fully vested in the plan. Forfeitures may be distributed to the other participants in the plan or used to offset employer contribution.

Form 1099R A form sent to the recipient of a plan distribution and filed with the IRS listing the amount of the distribution.

Form 5500 A form which all qualified retirement plans (excluding SEPs and SIMPLE IRAs) must file annually with the IRS.

graduated or graded vesting A vesting schedule in which the employee earns the right to employer contributions gradually over a period of years, for example 25 percent ownership each year for four years. (See also *vesting*.)

guaranteed investment contracts (GICs) Accounts that are invested in interest-bearing contracts purchased directly from banks, insurance companies, or mutual funds, which guarantee to maintain the value of the principle and all accumulated interest. Also called stable value funds, these accounts do not go down in value.

hardship or in-service distribution When a participant withdraws plan funds prior to retirement, at the employer's option. Eligibility for such distributions exists when financial hardship is present. These distributions are taxable as early distributions and are subject to a 10 percent early withdrawal federal income tax penalty if the participant is under age 59$\frac{1}{2}$.

highly compensated employee (HCE) An employee who received more than $90,000 in compensation in 2002 (indexed annually) or is a 5 percent owner in the company.

individual retirement account (IRA) Personal retirement vehicles in which a person can make annual tax deductible contributions. These accounts must meet IRS Code 408 requirements, but are created and funded at the discretion of the employee. They are not employer-sponsored plans.

Internal Revenue Service (IRS) This branch of the U.S. Treasury Department is responsible for administering the requirements of qualified pension plans and other retirement vehicles. The IRS also worked with the DOL and the PWBA to develop Form 5500, and is now responsible for monitoring the data submitted annually on Form 5500 reports.

Keogh plan A qualified defined-contribution plan permitting self-employed individuals to contribute a portion of their earnings pretax to an individual account.

KSOP A plan arrangement that includes both 401(k) contributions and an ESOP.

leased employee An individual employed by a leasing organization who provides contract services for the company for a period of more than one year.

lump-sum distribution The distribution of a participant's entire account balance within one calendar year due to retirement, death, or disability.

matching contribution A contribution made by the company to the account of the participant in ratio to contributions made by the participant.

material modification A change in the terms of the plan that may affect plan participants, or other changes in a summary plan document (SPD).

median market cap An indicator of the size of companies in which a fund invests.

money market fund A mutual fund seeking to generate income for participants through investments in short-term securities.

money-purchase plan A type of defined-contribution plan in which the employer's contributions are determined by a specific formula, usually as a percentage of pay. Contributions are not dependent on company profits. The benefit is the final account balance.

multiemployer plan A pension plan to which more than one employer contributes, and which is maintained according to collective bargaining agreements.

mutual fund An account with a broad range of investment options, each of which are diversified, reducing the risk to the participant.

named fiduciary A fiduciary named in the plan document that has them the authority to control and manage the operation of the plan. The named fiduciary must also be identified as a fiduciary by a procedure specified in the plan document.

nondiscrimination rules IRS rules that prohibit the plan or plan sponsor from giving disproportionately larger benefits to a highly compensated employee (HCE). Specific nondiscimination testing must be done to determine if plans have broken this rule and are top heavy.

nonelective contribution An employer contribution that cannot be withdrawn or paid to the employee in cash. This contribution is neither a matching contribution or an elective contribution.

non–highly compensated employee (NHCE) Employees who are not highly compensated. Generally they are employees who earned less than $90,000 in 2002 (indexed to inflation). See Highly compensated employee.

nonqualified deferred-compensation plan A plan subject to tax, in which the assets of certain employees (usually highly compensated employees) are deferred. These funds may be reached by an employer's creditors.

participant Person who has an account in the plan and any beneficiaries who may be eligible to receive an account balance.

participant-directed account A plan that allows participants to select their own investment options.

party-in-interest Those who are a party-in-interest to a plan include: the employer; the directors, officers, employees, or owners of the employer; any employee organization whose members are plan participants; plan fiduciaries; and plan service providers.

Pension and Welfare Benefits Administration (PWBA) This branch of the Department of Labor protects the pensions, health plans, and other employee benefits of American workers. The PWBA enforces Title I of ERISA, which contains rules for reporting and disclosure, vesting, participation, funding, and fiduciary conduct.

Pension Benefit Guaranty Corporation (PBGC) A federal agency established by Title IV of ERISA for the insurance of defined benefit pension plans. The PBGC provides payment of pension benefits if a plan terminates and is unable to cover all required benefits.

plan administrator The individual, group, or corporation named in the plan document as responsible for day-to-day operations. The plan sponsor is generally the plan administrator if no other entity is named.

plan document A document outlining the parameters under which a retirement plan will be operated. This document must be given to employees upon request.

plan loan Loan from a participant's accumulated plan assets, not to exceed 50 percent of the balance or $50,000, less the amount of any outstanding plan loans. This is an optional plan feature.

plan sponsor The entity responsible for establishing and maintaining the plan.

plan year The calendar, policy, or fiscal year for which plan records are maintained.

portability The ability of an employee, upon termination of employment, to transfer pension funds from one employer's plan to another without penalty.

preretirement survivor rights The right of a surviving beneficiary to receive benefits if vested plan participant dies before retirement.

price-book ratio The share price of a stock divided by its net worth, or book value, per share.

price-earnings (PE) ratio The ratio of a stock's current price to its earnings per share over the past year. The PE ratio of a fund is the weighted average of the PE ratios of the stocks it holds.

prohibited transaction Activities regarding treatment of plan assets by fiduciaries that are prohibited by ERISA. This includes transactions with a party-in-interest, including, sale, exchange, lease, or loan of plan securities or other properties.

profit sharing plan Company-sponsored plan funded only by company contributions. Company contributions may be determined by a fixed formula related to the employer's profits, or may be at the discretion of the board of directors.

prudent man rule ERISA fiduciary law that requires all fiduciaries to conduct the business of the plan with prudence and care. Any fiduciary violating this law is liable to the plan and its participants for all losses.

qualified domestic relations order (QDRO) A judgment, decree, or order that creates or recognizes the right of an alternate payee (such as former spouse, child, etc.) to receive all or a portion of a participant's retirement plan benefits.

qualified joint and survivor annuity (QJSA) An annuity with payments continuing to the surviving spouse after the participant's death, equal to at least 50 percent of the participant's benefit.

qualified plan Any plan that qualifies for favorable tax treatment by meeting the requirements of section 401(a) of the Internal Revenue Code and by following applicable regulations. Includes 401(k) and deferred profit sharing plans.

rollover The action of moving plan assets from one qualified plan to another or to an IRA within 60 days of distributions, while retaining the tax benefits of a qualified plan.

safe harbor rules Provisions that exempt certain individuals or kinds of companies from one or more regulations.

salary deduction Also known as payroll deduction. When a plan participant arranges to have pretax contributions made directly from his or her paycheck, it is arranged through salary deduction.

Savings Incentive Match Plan for Employees (SIMPLE plan) A type of defined-contribution plan for employers with 100 or fewer employees in which the employer matches employee deferrals up to 3 percent of compensation or provides nonelective contributions up to 2 percent of compensation. These contributions are immediately and 100 percent vested, and they are the only employer contribution to the plan. SIM-PLE plans may be structured as individual retirement accounts (IRAs) or as 401(k) plans.

service provider A company that provides any type of service to the plan, including managing assets, record keeping, providing plan education, and administering the plan.

Schedule SSA A form that must be filed by all plans subject to ERISA Section 203 minimum vesting requirements. The schedule, which is attached to Form 5500, provides data on participants who separated from service with a vested benefit but were not paid their benefits.

Simplified Employee-Pension Plan (SEP) A defined-contribution plan in which employers make contributions to individual employee accounts (similar to IRAs). Employees may also make pretax contributions to these accounts. As of January, 1997, no new SEP plans may be formed.

SIMPLE Plan See *Savings Incentive Match Plan for Employees.*

stock bonus plan A defined-contribution plan in which company contributions are distributable in the form of company stock.

summary annual report A report that companies must file annually on the financial status of the plan. The summary annual report must be automatically provided to participants every year.

summary plan description (SPD) A document describing the features of an employer-sponsored plan. The primary purpose of the SPD is to disclose the features of the plan to current and potential plan participants. ERISA requires that certain information be contained in the SPD, including participant rights under ERISA, claims procedures, and funding arrangements.

summary of material modifications A document that must be distributed to plan participants summarizing any material modifications made to a plan.

target-benefit plan A type of defined-contribution plan in which company contributions are based on an actuarial valuation designed to provide a target benefit to each participant upon retirement. The plan does not guarantee that such benefit will be paid; its only obligation is to pay whatever benefit can be provided by the amount in the participant's account. It is a hybrid of a money-purchase plan and a defined-benefit plan.

tax-sheltered annuity (TSA) See 403(b) plan.

top-heavy plan A plan in which 60 percent of account balances (both vested and nonvested) are held by certain highly compensated employees.

trustee The individual, bank, or trust company having fiduciary responsibility for holding plan assets.

turnover rate (of a fund) A measure of the trading activity in a mutual fund.

vesting The participant's ownership right to company contributions.

vesting schedule The structure for determining a participant's ownership right to company contributions (see *matching contributions*). In a plan with immediate vesting, participants own all company contributions as soon as they are deposited into individual accounts. In cliff vesting, company contributions will be fully owned (i.e., vested) only after a specific amount of time, and employees leaving before the allotted time are not entitled to any company contributions (with certain exceptions for retirees). In plans with graduated or graded vesting, vesting occurs in specified increments.

Spanish

acción Unidad individual de propiedad de valores o de un fondo de inversión.

acción común (acción) La unidad básica de propiedad en una corporación.

activo Cualquier cosa que usted posee que tiene un valor monetario.

asignación de activos Distribuir su cuenta entre clases de activos como acciones, bonos o inversiones a corto plaza.

beneficiario La persona que usted decide para recibir sus beneficios después de su fallecimiento.

bonos Una forma de IOU, emitido por una corporación, municipios, o el gobierno. El propietario de un bono recibe los pagos de interés durante de un periodo específico de tiempo.

capital principal La cantidad original de dinero que usted invierte en una inversión particular.

contribución La cantidad de su paga que está puesto en su 401(k). Este cantidad esta determinado antes de los impuestos.

clases de activos Los tipos de inversiónes diferentes. Acciónes, bonos o inversiónes a corto plazo son ejemplos de clases de activos.

diversificación El proceso de distribuir su dinero por diferentes tipos de inversiónes y companías debajo de la intenció de minimizar su riesgo.

interés El porcentaje de la capital principal (la cantidad original) que se le está pagando a usted durante el tiempo que su dinero está prestado.

inversión de rendimiento fijo Una inversión que paga una tasa de redimiento. Bonos y letras del tesoro son dos opciónes de inversión de redimento fijo.

opperaciónes bursátiles Comprar y vender valores.

patrimonio neto La propiedad que tiene en sus cuentas de inversión.

proceso de compuesto El proceso en que el dinero que usted invierte gane interés y estos ganandos siguen produciendo más interés.

redimiento Un punto de referencia para saber la ganacia o pérdida obtenida por una inversión.

valores Describir la posesión de acciones unidades o fondos di inversiónes.

volatilidad Una medida como una inversión aumenta o disminuye en valor.

Index

Take Control with Your 401(k)

For special discounts on 20 or more copies of *Take Control with Your 401(k)*, please call Dearborn Trade Special Sales at 800-621-9621, extension 4455.

Dearborn™
Trade Publishing
A **Kaplan Professional** Company